Weekly Assessments

Mc
Graw
Hill
Education

www.mheonline.com/readingwonders

Send all inquiries to:
McGraw-Hill Education
Two Penn Plaza
New York, New York 10121

ISBN: 978-0-07-677218-6
MHID: 0-07-677218-7

Printed in the United States of America.

2 3 4 5 6 7 8 9 RHR 20 19 18 17 16
B

Table of Contents

Table of Contents– Cont'd.

Teacher Introduction

Weekly Assessments

The *Weekly Assessment* is an integral part of the complete assessment program aligned with *Reading Wonders* and state standards.

Purpose of *Weekly Assessments*

Weekly Assessments offers the opportunity to monitor student progress in a steady and structured manner while providing formative assessment data. As students complete each week of the reading program, they will be assessed on their understanding of key instructional content. The results of the assessments can be used to inform subsequent instruction.

The results of *Weekly Assessments* a status of current achievement in relation to student progress through the curriculum.

Focus of *Weekly Assessments*

The focus of *Weekly Assessments* on two key areas of English Language Arts—Reading and Language. Students will read two selections each week and respond to items focusing on Comprehension Skills and Vocabulary Strategies. These items assess the ability to access meaning from the text and demonstrate understanding of unknown and multiple-meaning words and phrases.

Administering *Weekly Assessments*

Each weekly assessment should be administered once the instruction for the specific week is completed. Make copies of the weekly assessment for the class. You will need one copy of the Answer Key page for each student taking the assessment. The scoring table at the bottom of the Answer Key provides a place to list student scores. The accumulated data from each weekly assessment charts student progress and underscores strengths and weaknesses.

After each student has a copy of the assessment, provide a version of the following directions: **Say:** *Write your name and the date on the question pages for this assessment.* (When students are finished, continue with the directions.) *You will read two selections and answer questions about them. Read each selection and the questions that follow it carefully. For the multiple-choice items, completely fill in the circle next to the correct answer. For items that require a written response, write that response clearly in the space provided. For the constructed response item, write your response on the lines provided. When you have completed the assessment, put your pencil down and turn the pages over. You may begin now.*

Answer procedural questions during the assessment, but do not provide any assistance on the items or selections. After the class has completed the assessment, ask students to verify that their names and the date are written on the necessary pages.

Teacher Introduction

Overview of *Weekly Assessments*

Each weekly assessment is comprised of the following

- 2 "Cold Read" selections
- 10 items assessing Comprehension Skills and Vocabulary Strategies
- 1 constructed response item assessing Comprehension and the ability to write across texts

Reading Selections

Each weekly assessment features two selections on which the assessment items are based. (In instances where poetry is used, multiple poems may be set as a selection.) The selections reflect the unit theme and/or weekly Essential Question to support the focus of the classroom instruction. Because the weekly assessments have been composed to assess student application of the skills rather than genre or genre knowledge, selections are not always the same genre as the reading selections in the Literature Anthology or RWW.

Selections increase in complexity as the school year progresses to mirror the rigor of reading materials students encounter in the classroom. The Lexile goal by unit is as follows—Unit 1: 520L; Unit 2: 580L; Unit 3: 640L; Unit 4: 700L; Unit 5: 760L; and Unit 6: 820L.

Assessment Items

Weekly assessments feature the following item types—selected response (SR), multiple selected response (MSR), evidence-based selected response (EBSR), constructed response (CR), technology-enhanced constructed response (TECR), and extended constructed response (ECR). (Please note that the print versions of TECR items are available in this component; the full functionality of the items is available only through the online assessment.) This variety of item types provides multiple methods of assessing student understanding, allows for deeper investigation into skills and strategies, and provides students an opportunity to become familiar with the kinds of questions they will encounter in next generation assessments, both consortia-related and state-mandated.

Comprehension Items

Each selection is followed by items that assess student understanding of the text through the use of Comprehension Skills—both that week's Comprehension Skill focus and a review Comprehension Skill. The review skill is taken from a week as near as possible to the current week and aligns with the instruction.

Vocabulary Items

Each selection is followed by items that ask students to demonstrate the ability to uncover the meanings of unknown and multiple-meaning words and phrases using Vocabulary Strategies.

Comprehension—Extended Constructed Response

At the close of each weekly assessment is a constructed response item that provides students the opportunity to craft a written response that shows their critical thinking skills and allows them to support an opinion/position by using text evidence from one or both selections.

NOTE: Please consider this item as an optional assessment that allows students to show comprehension of a text in a more in-depth manner as they make connections between and within texts.

Teacher Introduction

Scoring *Weekly Assessments*

Items 1–10 are each worth two points, for a twenty-point assessment. Each part of a EBSR is worth 1 point; MSR and TECR items should be answered correctly in full, though you may choose to provide partial credit. If you decide to have students complete the constructed response, use the correct response parameters provided in the Answer Key along with the scoring rubric listed below to assign a score of 0 through 4.

Score: 4

- The student understands the question/prompt and responds suitably using the appropriate text evidence from the selection or selections.
- The response is an acceptably complete answer to the question/prompt.
- The organization of the response is meaningful.
- The response stays on-topic; ideas are linked to one another with effective transitions.
- The response has correct spelling, grammar, usage, and mechanics, and it is written neatly and legibly.

Score: 3

- The student understands the question/prompt and responds suitably using the appropriate text evidence from the selection or selections.
- The response is a somewhat complete answer to the question/prompt.
- The organization of the response is somewhat meaningful.
- The response maintains focus; ideas are linked to one another.
- The response has occasional errors in spelling, grammar, usage, and mechanics, and it is, for the most part, written neatly and legibly.

Score: 2

- The student has partial understanding of the question/prompt and uses some text evidence.
- The response is an incomplete answer to the question/prompt.
- The organization of the response is weak.
- The writing is careless; contains extraneous information and ineffective transitions.
- The response requires effort to read easily.
- The response has noticeable errors in spelling, grammar, usage, and mechanics, and it is written somewhat neatly and legibly.

Score: 1

- The student has minimal understanding of the question/prompt and uses little to no appropriate text evidence.
- The response is a barely acceptable answer to the question/prompt.
- The response lacks organization.
- The writing is erratic with little focus; ideas are not connected to each other.
- The response is difficult to follow.
- The response has frequent errors in spelling, grammar, usage, and mechanics, and it is written with borderline neatness and legibility.

Score: 0

- The student fails to compose a response.
- If a response is attempted, it is inaccurate, meaningless, or completely irrelevant.
- The response may be written so poorly that it is neither legible nor understandable.

Teacher Introduction

Evaluating Scores

The primary focus of each weekly assessment is to evaluate student progress toward mastery of previously-taught skills and strategies.

The expectation is for students to score 80% or higher on the assessment as a whole. Within this score, the expectation is for students to score 75% or higher on the items assessing Comprehension Skills; score 75% or higher on the items assessing the particular week's Vocabulary Strategy; and "3" or higher on the extended constructed response, if assigned.

For students who do not meet these benchmarks, assign appropriate lessons from the Tier 2 online PDFs. Refer to the weekly "Progress Monitoring" spreads in the Teacher's Editions of *Wonders* for specific lessons.

The Answer Keys in *Weekly Assessments* have been constructed to provide the information you need to aid your understanding of student performance, as well as individualized instructional and intervention needs. Further metadata is available in the online versions of the assessment, including specific test claims and targets.

This column lists the instructional content for the week that is assessed in each item.

Question	Correct Answer	Content Focus	CCSS	Complexity

This column lists alignment for each assessment item.

This column lists the Depth of Knowledge associated with each item.

Question	Correct Answer	Content Focus	CCSS	Complexity
7	B, E	Main Idea and Key Details	RI.3.2	DOK 2
8	D	Context Clues	L.3.4a	DOK 2
9A	C	Main Idea and Key Details	RI.3.2	DOK 2
9B	B	Main Idea and Key Details/Text Evidence	RI.3.2/RI.3.1	DOK 2

Although all items feature use of text evidence, this is explicitly mentioned in PART B EBSR items.

Comprehension 1A, 1B, 4, 5, 6, 7A, 7B, 10	/12	%
Vocabulary 2, 3A, 3B, 8, 9	/8	%
Total Weekly Assessment Score	/20	%

Scoring rows identify items associated with Reading and Language strands and allow for quick record keeping.

Read the passage "Singing Out" before answering Numbers 1 through 5.

Singing Out

Nina Martinez shut the classroom door behind her and walked down the hall. She trudged up the steps to the second floor. There was a reason why Nina felt nervous this morning. She could not believe that she had decided to try out for the talent show. She loved to sing, but she disliked singing in front of other people. "Why am I doing this?" Nina thought.

Taking a deep breath, she pushed open the door of the auditorium and went inside. The theater was filled with laughing children. Nina saw her friends Luz and James along with a few other students from her class.

The bright, sunny room left no place for her to hide. A few teachers sat on folding chairs. Seeing Mrs. Brent, her music teacher, made Nina even more nervous. The teachers waited for the children to settle down. There was the stage, cold and bare.

"Hi, Nina!" Luz called out. "I didn't think you would try out for the talent show. You are usually so timid and shy in front of a group of people."

GO ON →

"That's nonsense," Nina said. "I'm not shy at all."

Luz laughed, "Yeah, right." Then she chuckled as she ran off to find a seat. Nina followed, dragging her feet. She wished she were downstairs sitting quietly at her desk. What mess had she gotten herself into?

One by one the students got up on the stage and sang or played a musical instrument, and Nina was amazed at how confident her classmates seemed. "Nina Martinez!" a voice called out. It was Mrs. Brent, the music teacher. Nina jumped from her chair when she heard Mrs. Brent announce her name. Nina felt small as she walked to the enormous, empty stage. It was huge! Her face was hot, and her shaking hands were as cold as ice. She fumbled with the sheet music of her favorite song. She tried to sing, but the words would not come out.

"I–I–" Nina began, and then stopped. "I can't," she said softly.

"Close your eyes and pretend you are alone," said Mrs. Brent gently. "Forget about everyone else and just sing to please yourself."

Nina felt silly, but she gave it a try. She shut her eyes and raised her voice and sang out. To Nina's surprise, her hands stopped shaking and the song poured out like honey from a jar.

Nina heard Mrs. Brent clap and applaud loudly at the end of her song. "That's the first time I have actually heard your voice," she said. "You have such a beautiful voice. You are in the show!"

Nina let out a big sigh and smiled happily. Singing in front of people wasn't so bad, after all.

GO ON →

Name: _Kaliyh ._ Date: _____

Now answer Numbers 1 through 5. Base your answers on "Singing Out."

1 This question has two parts. First, answer part A. Then, answer part B.

Part A: Read the sentences from the passage.

Taking a deep breath, she pushed open the door of the <u>auditorium</u> and went inside. The theater was filled with laughing children.

What does <u>auditorium</u> **most likely** mean?

Ⓐ a friendly, open person

Ⓑ a small space in a house

Ⓒ a room for performances

Ⓓ a pantry for food

Part B: Which word helps you understand what <u>auditorium</u> means?

Ⓐ breath

Ⓑ laughing

Ⓒ door

Ⓓ theater

2 This question has two parts. First, answer part A. Then, answer part B.

Part A: Why does Nina feel nervous the first time she tries to sing?

(A) She does not get along with Mrs. Brent.

(B) She cannot remember the words to her song.

(C) She cannot see the words on her music sheet.

(D) She does not like to perform in front of people.

Part B: What text evidence shows why Nina feels nervous?

(A) "She loved to sing, but she disliked singing in front of other people."

(B) "She fumbled with the sheet music of her favorite song."

(C) "She tried to sing, but the words would not come out."

(D) "Nina jumped from her chair when she heard Mrs. Brent announce her name."

3 Read the sentences from the passage.

Luz laughed, "Yeah, right." Then she chuckled as she ran off to find a seat.

Which word helps you understand what chuckled means?

(A) laughed

(B) ran

(C) right

(D) seat

GO ON →

4 When Mrs. Brent tells Nina to just sing for herself, what does it show about Mrs. Brent? Pick **two** choices.

(A) She wants Nina to do well.

(B) She thinks Nina's voice is too soft.

(C) She does not think Nina will be in the show.

(D) She does not think Nina will remember the song.

(E) She understands why Nina feels nervous.

5 Nina is proud of herself at the end of the story. Underline the **two** details that **best** support this conclusion.

Nina heard Mrs. Brent clap and applaud loudly at the end of her song. "That's the first time I have actually heard your voice," she said. "You have such a beautiful voice. You are in the show!"

Nina let out a big sigh and smiled happily. Singing in front of people wasn't so bad, after all.

GO ON →

Read the passage "New Kid in School" before answering Numbers 6 through 10.

New Kid in School

Jayden watched the kids play from his corner of the school playground. Some were swinging on the swings or sliding down the slide. Others were kicking a dirty old soccer ball around. It was his third day at his new school and his third recess period standing in the corner of the playground, alone. He wished someone would ask him to swing, slide, or play soccer, but no one did. That day after school, Jayden walked home slowly with his head down. As he passed the park, shouting and laughing caught his attention.

"Over here!" someone shouted. "Kick it! Kick it to me!" someone hollered. It was some neighborhood kids playing soccer. Jayden stopped to watch them and recognized several of his classmates. He paused a few minutes to observe them. He was hoping they would see him and invite him to join their game, but no one did.

Jayden missed his old school and his old friends. "Why did we have to move?" he muttered to himself and whispered under his breath. "I don't have any friends here. I'll never have any friends here. Back home, I had Shawn, Jorge, and Nora. Back home, I—" Jayden caught himself. This was his home now, whether he liked it or not.

When he reached his house, it appeared empty. "Mom?" he called out, walking from room to room. "Mom? I'm home." Then he noticed a note attached to the refrigerator. It read: "Barry and I are across the street at our neighbor's house. Come on over, honey."

In the neighbor's backyard, Jayden saw his mother talking with a woman. They were chatting over cups of tea at a patio table. His three-year-old brother Barry and a little girl about the same age were playing in a sandbox.

GO ON →

"Hi, sweetie!" his mother called. "How was school today?"

"Okay," Jayden replied, though it hadn't been.

"This is our neighbor, Mrs. Ori, and her little girl Ava."

Just then, Ava reached out and grabbed the toy car at Barry's feet.

"Uh-oh," Jayden thought. "Look out!"

The car was Barry's favorite toy, and if anybody else touched it, he would wail and cry and kick, but the wail and the kicks didn't happen. Instead, Barry watched Ava roll the car through the sand. Then he picked up a toy truck and did the same.

That night in bed, Jayden did some thinking. "Maybe I've been going at this friends business the wrong way. I've been waiting for people to make friends with me. Maybe I should try to make friends with them," he said to himself. The next day on the playground, he approached Tyler, one of the soccer players he'd seen the day before.

"Hi," Jayden smiled. "I got this new soccer ball for my birthday a few weeks ago. Do you want to use it instead of that old mushy one?"

"Sure!" Tyler answered.

"Do you want to be on my side? What position do you play?"

Out loud, Jayden said, "I play forward." To himself, he said, "Whoever thought I could learn something from my three-year-old brother!"

GO ON →

Now answer Numbers 6 through 10. Base your answers on "New Kid in School."

6 Read the sentences from the passage. Circle the sentence that **best** tells you how Jayden feels about the move.

Jayden stopped to watch them and recognized several of his classmates.

He was hoping they would see him and invite him to join their game, but no one did.

He paused a few minutes to observe them.

Jayden missed his old school and his old friends.

7 This question has two parts. First, answer part A. Then, answer part B.

Part A: Read the sentence from the passage.

"Why did we have to move?" he <u>muttered</u> to himself and whispered under his breath.

What does <u>muttered</u> **most likely** mean?

(A) to shout loudly so everyone can hear

(B) to use words that make no sense

(C) to say something in a low voice

(D) to be completely quiet

Part B: Which word helps you understand what <u>muttered</u> means?

(A) himself   (C) under

(B) move   (D) whispered

GO ON →

8 Read the sentence from the passage.

The car was Barry's favorite toy, and if anybody else touched it, he would <u>wail</u> and cry and kick, but the <u>wail</u> and the kicks didn't happen.

Which word helps you understand what <u>wail</u> means?

(A) anybody

(B) cry

(C) favorite

(D) touched

9 How does Jayden feel because of his brother's success at making a new friend? Pick **two** choices.

(A) His mother was wrong.

(B) No one at school likes him.

(C) He needs to try harder to make friends.

(D) He should make friends with his brother.

(E) Friends can have something in common.

GO ON →

10 This question has two parts. First, answer part A. Then, answer part B.

Part A: Which word **best** describes Jayden at the end of the story?

(A) happy

(B) pushy

(C) shy

(D) upset

Part B: What text evidence supports how Jayden feels at the end of the story?

(A) "He wished someone would ask him to swing, slide, or play soccer, but no one did."

(B) "'I don't have any friends here. I'll never have any friends here.'"

(C) "This was his home now, whether he liked it or not."

(D) "'Whoever thought I could learn something from my three-year-old brother!'"

Now answer Number 11. Base your answer on "Singing Out" and "New Kid in School."

11 How are Nina and Jayden alike at the beginning of the passages? How are they alike at the end?

_____

_____

_____

_____

_____

_____

_____

_____

_____

_____

_____

_____

Answer Key

Question	Correct Answer	Content Focus	CCSS	Complexity
1A	C	Synonyms	L.3.4a	DOK 2
1B	C	Synonyms/Text Evidence	L.3.4a RL.3.1	DOK 2
2A	D	Character, Setting, Plot: Character	RL.3.3	DOK 3
2B	A	Character, Setting, Plot: Character/ Text Evidence	RL.3.3 RL.3.1	DOK 3
3	A	Synonyms	L.3.4a	DOK 2
4	A, E	Character, Setting, Plot: Character	RL.3.3	DOK 3
5	see below	Character, Setting, Plot: Character	RL.3.3	DOK 3
6	see below	Character, Setting, Plot: Character	RL.3.3	DOK 2
7A	C	Synonyms	L.3.4a	DOK 2
7B	D	Synonyms/Text Evidence	L.3.4a RL.3.1	DOK 2
8	B	Synonyms	L.3.4a	DOK 2
9	C, E	Character, Setting, Plot: Character	RL.3.3	DOK 3
10A	A	Character, Setting, Plot: Character	RL.3.3	DOK 3
10B	D	Character, Setting, Plot: Character/Text Evidence	RL.3.3 RL.3.1	DOK 3
11	see below	Writing About Text	W.3.8	DOK 4

Comprehension 2A, 2B, 4, 5, 6, 9, 10A, 10B	/12	%
Vocabulary 1A, 1B, 3, 7A, 7B, 8	/8	%
Total Weekly Assessment Score	/20	%

5 Students should underline the following sentences:
- Nina let out a big sigh and smiled happily.
- Singing in front of people wasn't so bad, after all.

6 Students should circle the following sentence:
- Jayden missed his old school and his old friends.

11 To receive full credit for the response, the following information should be included: Both are unhappy at the beginning. Nina is nervous, and Jayden is lonely. Both are happy at the end. Nina has learned a trick to make her confident enough to sing, and Jayden has learned how to make new friends.

Read the passage "A Lesson Learned" before answering Numbers 1 through 5.

A Lesson Learned

There once lived a wealthy man named Katu. Because he was so rich, he only wanted the finest things in life. He thought everything he owned was the best. He made sure the people in his village knew it.

Katu believed his home was not good enough for him. He wanted a house bigger and better than anyone else in the village. So, one day he decided to build a new house with the tallest logs he could find. He bragged to everyone that his logs were the best money could buy.

Katu needed a sturdy elephant to move the heavy logs to build his house. He hired a man who owned an elephant named Lago. Lago was the strongest elephant anyone from the village had ever seen. All the villagers watched how easily Lago piled the heavy logs on top of each other to build the house. They were amazed by his strength. Katu watched as Lago piled the logs higher and higher. Katu began bragging about his house to two men who were standing nearby.

GO ON →

"You see, my friends," said Katu, "how wonderful my house will be. There will be no other house like it in the village. My house will be the best house in the village."

Katu continued to brag about Lago's strength and his house to the two other men. But there was something about the powerful elephant that Katu did not know. Lago understood every word that Katu said. The elephant did not like what he heard. Lago decided that he had heard enough. Katu was still bragging when one of the men interrupted him. The man pointed over Katu's shoulder.

"What is it?" Katu asked angrily. "Can't you see I am busy?"

Katu tried to ignore the man, but the man kept pointing. Katu finally turned around and stopped talking. Lago was coming straight at him! The two men quickly scrambled out of the way. Katu was too afraid to move. Lago seized Katu with his trunk and lifted him high in the air. The elephant held Katu over his new house. Then Lago ran into the house as hard as he could. The house swayed and collapsed into a heap of logs. Lago backed away from the fallen house. He set Katu gently on the ground.

It took Katu many weeks to rebuild his house, but he learned his lesson. From that day on, he promised to never brag again.

GO ON →

Name: _____ Date: _____

Now answer Numbers 1 through 5. Base your answers on "A Lesson Learned."

1 Read the sentence from the passage.

Katu needed a <u>sturdy</u> elephant to move the heavy logs to build his house.

What does <u>sturdy</u> **most likely** mean in the sentence above?

(A) friendly   (C) strong

(B) smart   (D) young

2 This question has two parts. First, answer part A. Then, answer part B.

Part A: Read the sentences from the passage.

The two men quickly <u>scrambled</u> out of the way. Katu was too afraid to move.

What does the word <u>scrambled</u> mean?

(A) hurried

(B) searched

(C) skipped

(D) walked

Part B: Which word helps you understand what <u>scrambled</u> means?

(A) two

(B) quickly

(C) afraid

(D) move

GO ON →

3 What happens **after** Katu brags to the two men but **before** Lago runs into Katu's house?

Ⓐ Lago holds Katu over the house.

Ⓑ Katu promises to never brag again.

Ⓒ Katu's house collapses into a heap of logs.

Ⓓ Lago piles the heavy logs on top of each other to build the house.

4 Put the events of the passage in the correct order by numbering them from 1 to 5. Write the correct number in front of each event.

_____	Lago runs into Katu's house, causing it to fall apart into a heap of logs.
_____	Katu wants to build the biggest house in the village.
_____	Katu brags about the house and Lago's strength.
_____	Lago does not like hearing Katu's bragging.
_____	Katu hires a man who owns the strongest elephant in the village.

GO ON →

5 This question has two parts. First, answer part A. Then, answer part B.

Part A: What kind of man is Katu at the end of the story?

(A) a wiser man

(B) a richer man

(C) a braver man

(D) a stronger man

Part B: What text evidence supports your answer in part A?

(A) "It took Katu many weeks to rebuild his house, but he learned his lesson."

(B) "He bragged to everyone that his logs were the best money could buy."

(C) "Because he was so rich, he only wanted the finest things in life."

(D) "Katu was too afraid to move."

GO ON →

Read the passage "The Ship of the Desert" before answering Numbers 6 through 10.

The Ship of the Desert

Long, long ago, a man was traveling on the edge of the desert. He carried food and water on his back. He lugged his heavy tent on the ground behind him. The man was returning to his family far away, but the hot sun and his heavy load made the journey difficult.

Suddenly, he saw a strange creature ahead of him. It was large, brown, and hairy. The creature bellowed at him, and the loud noise frightened him! The man rushed away. He ran as fast as he could, even with his heavy load.

The next day, he came across a similar creature. This time, the creature was at the far end of a small pool of water. It kept drinking and drinking. Curious, the man carefully inched closer to get a better look. The creature had long, skinny legs and a long, thick neck. Most remarkably, it had a huge hump on its back.

The third day, the man saw more and more of these odd creatures. He decided to observe them carefully to see what he could learn. They ate plants and drank water for long periods of time. Sometimes one would look up and stare straight at him. Another might even bellow, like the first creature he saw. But the man realized that the stares and bellows from the creatures were not mean. The creatures were actually meek and gentle.

GO ON →

The man watched some creatures coming over a high sand dune. He knew the desert extended for miles and miles past that dune. "These creatures must be able to walk in the desert without water for a long time!" he thought.

On the fourth day, the man came across one of the gentle giants. It was down in the sand with its eyes closed, dozing. The man had an idea.

"Perhaps this creature could help me carry my load," he thought. So he walked quietly up to the animal. He slipped a rope around its mouth and back over its ears. Then he loaded all of his belongings onto the creature's back and slipped onto its hump.

The animal awoke and got to its feet. The man rode it all the way home. His children greeted him excitedly. They too wanted to ride the wonderful creature.

"Now we can make the desert our home!" the man said happily. And that is how the camel came to be humans' great helper. And that is why we call it "The Ship of the Desert."

GO ON →

Now answer Numbers 6 through 10. Base your answers on "The Ship of the Desert."

6 This question has two parts. First, answer part A. Then, answer part B.

Part A: Read the sentences from the passage.

He carried food and water on his back. He <u>lugged</u> his heavy tent on the ground behind him.

What does the word <u>lugged</u> mean?

- Ⓐ bounced
- Ⓑ kicked
- Ⓒ pulled
- Ⓓ smashed

Part B: Which word helps you understand what <u>lugged</u> means?

- Ⓐ tent
- Ⓑ carried
- Ⓒ ground
- Ⓓ back

GO ON →

7 How does the sequence of events help you understand the passage? Pick **two** choices.

(A) The story is organized so that each day, the man has a different thought.

(B) It shows that the man wants to ride the camel on the first day.

(C) The man slowly gains knowledge by the end of the story.

(D) The camel refuses to help the man on the third day.

(E) The last day shows how the man learns nothing about the animal.

8 Read the sentence from the passage.

It was down in the sand with its eyes closed, dozing.

What does dozing mean in the sentence above?

(A) digging

(B) drinking

(C) eating

(D) sleeping

9 What happens after the man rides the creature all the way home?

(A) His children greet him excitedly.

(B) The creature falls asleep in the sand.

(C) The creature bellows at the man and frightens him.

(D) He watches some creatures walk over a high sand dune.

GO ON →

Name: _____ Date: _____

10 Put the events of the passage in the correct order by numbering them from 1 to 5. Write the correct number in front of each event.

	The man rides the animal all the way home.

	The man walks through the desert to return to his family.

	The man sees a creature that scares him.

	The man realizes the animals don't need water for a long time.

	The man watches these animals and learns about them.

Name: _____ Date: _____

Now answer Number 11. Base your answer on "A Lesson Learned" and "The Ship of the Desert."

11 Each of these passages is told through a series of events. Give details to show how Katu and the man in the desert change during the events in the passages.

_____

_____

_____

_____

_____

_____

_____

_____

_____

_____

_____

_____

Answer Key

Question	Correct Answer	Content Focus	CCSS	Complexity
1	C	Context Clues: Sentence Clues	L.3.4a	DOK 2
2	A	Context Clues: Sentence Clues	L.3.4a	DOK 2
3	A	Character, Setting, Plot: Sequence	RL.3.3	DOK 2
4	see below	Character, Setting, Plot: Sequence	RL.3.3	DOK 3
5A	A	Character, Setting, Plot: Sequence	RL.3.3	DOK 2
5B	A	Character, Setting, Plot: Sequence/Text Evidence	RL.3.3 RL.3.1	DOK 2
6A	C	Context Clues: Sentence Clues	L.3.4a	DOK 2
6B	D	Context Clues: Sentence Clues/Text Evidence	L.3.4a RL.3.1	DOK 2
7	A, C	Character, Setting, Plot: Sequence	RL.3.3	DOK 3
8	D	Context Clues: Sentence Clues	L.3.4a	DOK 2
9	A	Character, Setting, Plot: Sequence	RL.3.3	DOK 2
10	see below	Character, Setting, Plot: Sequence	RL.3.3	DOK 3
11	see below	Writing About Text	W.3.8	DOK 3

Comprehension 3, 4, 5A, 5B, 7, 9, 10	/12	%
Vocabulary 1, 2, 6A, 6B, 8	/8	%
Total Weekly Assessment Score	/20	%

4 Students should put the events in the following order:
- 1 - Katu wants to build the biggest house in the village.
- 2 - Katu hires a man who owns the strongest elephant in the village.
- 3 - Katu brags about the house and Lago's strength.
- 4 - Lago does not like hearing Katu's bragging.
- 5 - Lago runs into Katu's house, causing it to fall apart into a heap of logs.

10 Students should put the events in the following order:
- 1 - The man walks through the desert to return to his family.
- 2 - The man sees a creature that scares him.
- 3 - The man watches these animals and learns about them.
- 4 - The man realizes the animals don't need water for a long time.
- 5 - The man rides the animal all the way home.

11 To receive full credit for the response, the following information should be included: Katu thinks everything he owns is the best. He brags about his logs, how wonderful his house will be, and Lago's strength. Lago does not like what he hears and decides to teach him a lesson by knocking his house down. Katu realizes no one likes a bragger and promises never to do it again. The man in the desert observes unusual creatures and discovers the camels are actually meek and gentle. He uses them to carry him and his belongings, and realizes his family can make the desert their home.

Read the article "City of Parades" before answering Numbers 1 through 5.

City of Parades

Chicago is a big city. People from many different countries have come to live here. All these people are proud of their cultures. Every year they show their pride by marching in parades to celebrate their cultures. Many spectators fill the sidewalks to cheer on the people in the parade.

The first parade every year is the Chinese New Year Parade. It celebrates the first day of the Chinese calendar. The parade is held in January or February. People line the streets to watch the lion and dragon dancers, magicians, and acrobats. The parade ends with a huge, long paper dragon. People carry it on poles. Noisy firecrackers are set off as the dragon winds down the street.

Next comes the Saint Patrick's Day Parade. It happens in March. People march down the street with bagpipes. They play Irish songs. There are also marching bands, floats, and dancers. The dancers do the Irish jig. It is a tradition to wear green on Saint Patrick's Day. Even the Chicago River is green this day! People pour green dye into the river to make it green.

Just a few days later, people from Iran have a parade. They call the day Nowruz. It marks their New Year. Nowruz falls on the first day of spring. People place pink and purple flowers on the roadside. Children carry pinwheels shaped like flowers. People carry long signs that say, "Happy Nowruz!" Later in the day, many families get together for a holiday dinner.

Next is the Greek Independence Day Parade. This parade is held to celebrate Greece's freedom. People wave blue and white Greek flags as they march down the street. Men dress like army guards. They wear red caps and white skirts. They also wear red shoes that have big black balls of fur on the toes.

GO ON →

The Fifth of May Parade comes after the Greek parade. Mexican Americans call this day Cinco de Mayo. This parade is held to celebrate the day Mexico won an important battle. Red, white, and green floats parade down the street. Men and women in colorful costumes dance. Bands blow their horns and play their guitars. In fact, Mexican Americans have two parades each year. They also have a parade in September to celebrate their freedom.

The Columbus Day Parade is held in October. The parade celebrates Christopher Columbus's journey and the Italian-American culture. Italian Americans show their pride by playing music and performing dances from their country. It is the last cultural parade of the year.

All of these cultures make Chicago a very interesting place to live.

GO ON →

Now answer Numbers 1 through 5. Base your answers on "City of Parades."

1 Read the sentence from the article.

People place pink and purple flowers on the <u>roadside</u>.

Based on the words *road* and *side*, what is the meaning of the compound word <u>roadside</u>?

- (A) the side of a road
- (B) a road with two sides
- (C) the side of a driveway
- (D) a road that goes sideways

2 Which **three** words from the article are compound words?

- (A) bagpipes
- (B) cultures
- (C) firecrackers
- (D) sidewalks
- (E) traditions
- (F) parades

GO ON →

3 This question has two parts. First, answer part A. Then, answer part B.

Part A: What is the paper dragon in the Chinese New Year Parade a sign of?

- (A) The acrobats are coming.
- (B) The parade is about to end.
- (C) The lion dancers are coming.
- (D) The parade is about to begin.

Part B: Underline the sentence from the passage that **best** supports your answer in part A.

The first parade every year is the Chinese New Year Parade. It celebrates the first day of the Chinese calendar. The parade is held in January or February. People line the streets to watch the lion and dragon dancers, magicians, and acrobats. The parade ends with a huge, long paper dragon. People carry it on poles. Noisy firecrackers are set off as the dragon winds down the street.

GO ON →

4 This question has two parts. First, answer part A. Then, answer part B.

Part A: Why does the author talk about the Columbus Day Parade at the end of the article?

(A) It has the most spectators.

(B) It is the least important parade.

(C) it is the final parade of the year.

(D) It has the fewest floats in the parade.

Part B: What text evidence supports your answer in part A?

(A) The Columbus Day Parade takes place in October.

(B) The parade celebrates Italian-American culture.

(C) Italian Americans play music and perform dances.

(D) The Columbus Day Parade is the last cultural parade of the year.

5 How does the author organize the article to show that Chicago is the city of parades?

(A) by explaining how each parade started

(B) by comparing and contrasting each of the parades

(C) by telling the sequence in which the parades happen

(D) by telling the number of people that take part in the parades

GO ON →

Read the article "Pasta Comes to America" before answering Numbers 6 through 10.

Pasta Comes to America

Many Americans like pasta. They enjoy making and eating pasta dishes. Pasta can be long and thin. It can be short and thick. It can even come in shapes like wheels or stars. The names of different types of pasta often describe the way the noodle looks. For example, the word *spaghetti* means "little strings" in Italian. Some people eat pasta with cheese sauce or tomato sauce. Others love it with meat sauce or even just a little oil.

People who like pasta can thank Italian Americans. They helped bring pasta to America. Italians first came to America more than one hundred years ago. Many Italians came to live in the big cities in America. Often they would live together in their own neighborhoods. That is why many big cities today have a neighborhood called "Little Italy."

Italians loved many things about America. But they did not always like the food in their new country. They missed the food from Italy. They especially missed pasta. They liked the hard cheeses that they could cook with pasta. They grew vegetables and spices in their gardens. They would add fresh vegetables and spices to their sauces and pasta. They also liked fruit. They would eat it with pasta.

This was a different way of eating than most Americans were used to. They did not often use fresh fruits and vegetables in their cooking. And pasta was new to them, too.

Italian Americans found ways to get the foods they liked. First, they planted vegetables and spices in their own gardens. Then, they bought cheeses and pasta that came from faraway Italy.

GO ON →

Then war broke out. Pasta and cheese could not be shipped all the way from Italy. Pasta factories began to open in America. They could make the pasta that Italians wanted.

As a result, there was a lot of pasta being made in America. It did not cost much money to buy. Then it was discovered that pasta was healthy. Recipes for homemade pasta meals were included in cookbooks and magazines. Americans began to eat pasta at mealtimes in their homes. Spaghetti and meatballs became a favorite meal.

Italian Americans started to open pasta restaurants. They called them spaghetti houses. Italian restaurants soon became very popular restaurants. People liked these restaurants. It made them feel like they were in Italy. Even today, Americans enjoy eating at Italian restaurants.

GO ON →

Now answer Numbers 6 through 10. Base your answers on "Pasta Comes to America."

6 How does the author organize "Pasta Comes to America"?

Ⓐ by comparing Italian foods to other foods

Ⓑ by describing the foods Italian Americans enjoyed

Ⓒ by listing the order of events that led to Italian food's popularity

Ⓓ by explaining how Italian Americans were able to find the food they wanted

7 Read the sentence from the article.

Recipes for homemade pasta meals were included in cookbooks and magazines.

Based on the words *home* and *made*, what is the meaning of the compound word homemade?

Ⓐ materials used to build a home, such as wood or brick

Ⓑ made at home, rather than in a store or factory

Ⓒ family dinners served at home, rather than in a restaurant

Ⓓ different types of homes, such as ranches or log cabins

GO ON →

8 How does the author help the reader understand how Americans came to love pasta?

Ⓐ by comparing Italian food to American food

Ⓑ by giving the reasons why Italians eat pasta

Ⓒ by explaining how eating pasta helped Americans

Ⓓ by telling what happened once Italians moved to America

9 This question has two parts. First, answer part A. Then, answer part B.

Part A: How does the author explain the opening of American pasta factories?

Ⓐ The factories were the cause for war breaking out.

Ⓑ The factories were a contrast to the Italian factories.

Ⓒ The factories were the reason Italian restaurants became popular.

Ⓓ The factories were a key step in how Italians found the food they wanted.

Part B: Which sentence from the article **best** supports your answer in part A?

Ⓐ "They could make the pasta that Italians wanted."

Ⓑ "Then it was discovered that pasta was healthy."

Ⓒ "Italian Americans started to open pasta restaurants."

Ⓓ "Then, they bought cheeses and pasta that came from faraway Italy."

GO ON →

10 Which **three** words from the article are compound words?

Ⓐ vegetables

Ⓑ cookbooks

Ⓒ factories

Ⓓ gardens

Ⓔ mealtimes

Ⓕ meatballs

Now answer Number 11. Base your answer on "Pasta Comes to America."

11 How did pasta come to America? Your answer should include at least **three** key events, in order, from the article.

_____

_____

_____

_____

_____

_____

_____

_____

_____

_____

_____

_____

_____

_____

Answer Key

Name: _____

Question	Correct Answer	Content Focus	CCSS	Complexity
1	A	Compound Words	RI.3.4	DOK 1
2	A, C, D	Compound Words	RI.3.4	DOK 1
3A	B	Text Structure: Sequence	RI.3.8	DOK 2
3B	see below	Text Structure: Sequence/Text Evidence	RI.3.8 RI.3.1	DOK 2
4A	C	Text Structure: Sequence	RI.3.8	DOK 2
4B	D	Text Structure: Sequence/Text Evidence	RI.3.8 RI.3.1	DOK 2
5	C	Text Structure: Sequence	RI.3.8	DOK 2
6	C	Text Structure: Sequence	RI.3.8	DOK 2
7	B	Compound Words	RI.3.4	DOK 1
8	D	Text Structure: Sequence	RI.3.8	DOK 2
9A	D	Text Structure: Sequence	RI.3.8	DOK 2
9B	A	Text Structure: Sequence/Text Evidence	RI.3.8 RI.3.1	DOK 2
10	B, E, F	Compound Words	RI.3.4	DOK 1
11	see below	Writing About Text	W.3.8	DOK 3

Comprehension 3A, 3B, 4A, 4B, 5, 6, 8, 9A, 9B	/12	%
Vocabulary 1, 2, 7, 10	/8	%
Total Weekly Assessment Score	/20	%

3B Students should underline the following sentence:
  • The parade ends with a huge, long paper dragon.

11 To receive full credit for the response, three events should be included in order: Italians began coming to America from Italy. They did not like American food. They planted vegetables and spices in their own garden, and bought cheeses and pasta from Italy to add to their pasta. Pasta factories began to open up because they were not able to get pasta shipped from Italy.

Read the article "Helping Each Other" before answering Numbers 1 through 5.

Helping Each Other

Long ago, many people lived on farms. Sometimes farmers would need a new barn. So they asked their neighbors to come help build it. The event was known as a barn raising. People from all around traveled to a barn raising. Many times, the whole family got to go.

Everyone worked together to build a barn. It was a huge mountain to climb. Back then there were no machines to do the heavy jobs. People used hand tools, like saws, hammers, and shovels, to get the job done. Those who could not help build the barn had other jobs. Some people might watch the children while others would cook all the food. The farm was a beehive of activity.

There were many reasons why neighbors helped at a barn raising. First, people wanted to help those in need. If they could lend a hand, they would. Their help was a gift to their neighbor. Also, building a barn was hard work. The job was easier when more people joined together. Farmers would go the extra mile to get the job done and the barn would be finished more quickly. Finally, the neighbors knew that they might need a new barn someday. If they helped a farmer build a barn, that farmer could be counted on to help at their barn raising. In other words, the farmer would return the favor.

GO ON →

A barn raising was not all work, though. Everyone had fun. Most of the time, farm life was lonely because the farms were far apart. A family could go months without seeing another person. Building a barn brought lots of families together and gave them a chance to visit. Old friends got to talk with each other and catch up on the events that had taken place in their lives. People also made new friends. Young children ran and played together. Of course, everyone looked forward to the barn being completed. They often celebrated by throwing a big party. On the last night, everyone ate good food and laughed. They also played music and games.

Over time, some people left their farms. They wanted to live closer together, so they began moving into small towns. The people did not forget why they went to a barn raising, though. Small town neighbors worked together to make buildings that everyone could use. That is how a town got a schoolhouse or a courthouse built. Being a good neighbor in a small town made a big difference. It helped small towns blossom.

GO ON →

Now answer Numbers 1 through 5. Base your answers on "Helping Each Other."

1 This question has two parts. First, answer part A. Then, answer part B.

Part A: Which sentence gives the **best** reason why people attended a barn raising?

Ⓐ They had lots of experience building houses.

Ⓑ They enjoyed being surrounded by nature.

Ⓒ They needed to give their children something to do.

Ⓓ They wanted to help people in their community.

Part B: Underline the **three** sentences from the article that **best** support your answer in part A.

There were many reasons why neighbors helped at a barn raising. First, people wanted to help those in need. If they could lend a hand, they would. Their help was a gift to their neighbor. Also, building a barn was hard work. The job was easier when more people joined together.

2 Read the sentence from the article.

The farm was a beehive of activity.

What does the sentence mean?

Ⓐ The farm had beehives.

Ⓑ There was not much activity on the farm.

Ⓒ People on the farm were very busy.

Ⓓ Not everyone on the farm had a job to do.

GO ON →

3 Why does the author tell the reader that farm life was lonely?

(A) to explain why people lived far apart

(B) to explain why people moved to the city

(C) to explain why people built schoolhouses

(D) to explain why people went to a barn raising

4 Read the sentences from the article.

Everyone worked together to build a barn. It was <u>a huge mountain to climb</u>.

Why does the author compare building a barn to climbing a mountain?

(A) to show that it was hard to build a barn

(B) to show that barns could not be moved

(C) to show that barns looked heavy and tall

(D) to show that it was dangerous to climb up a barn

GO ON →

5 At the end of the passage, why does the author write about life in small towns? Pick **two** choices.

Ⓐ to compare barns with schoolhouses

Ⓑ to list the steps in building a courthouse

Ⓒ to state that people liked farm life better

Ⓓ to show how farm customs continued in towns

Ⓔ to explain why people started leaving farms

GO ON →

Read the article "Stopping Traffic" before answering Numbers 6 through 10.

Stopping Traffic

Garrett Morgan was born in 1877 in Paris, Kentucky. His parents were former slaves. He grew up on a farm, but Morgan knew that farm life was not for him. He left the farm when he was a teenager to seek better opportunities.

In 1895, Morgan moved to Cleveland, Ohio. He found a job fixing sewing machines. He loved working with the machines. He found new ways to make the machines better, and the news of his skills traveled fast.

In 1907, Morgan opened his own sewing equipment and repair shop. Soon his business shot up. It was time to expand. In 1909, he opened his own tailoring shop. It sold coats, suits and dresses. Everything was sewn with the machines he had made himself. As the years went by, Morgan's success and respect grew. He became an important person in the city of Cleveland.

Morgan's mind was a whirlwind. He was always thinking about what he could do next. He invented many things. In 1912, he invented a gas mask, which he called a safety hood. It allowed people to breathe clean air when there was a lot of smoke. He thought it would help firefighters do their job.

In 1916, Morgan used his invention. There was an explosion that trapped workers building a tunnel underground. There was a lot of smoke. Morgan and a team of volunteers used his gas masks to help save some of them. Morgan later received requests from fire departments that wanted to purchase the gas masks. His gas mask was later updated for use by the U.S. Army. The U.S. soldiers used them during the First World War. Morgan won a gold medal for his invention of the gas mask.

GO ON →

During this time, the streets of Cleveland were a circus. It was common for bicycles, horse-pulled wagons, and cars to share the same streets. There were some traffic signals on the streets. But they had only two signals: stop and go. This was not the only problem. Someone had to change the signal from stop to go by hand. If the person forgot to change the signal, there were accidents. Wrecks were common. Also, there was no time between stop and go. That caused a lot of accidents too.

One day Morgan saw a bad accident. An automobile hit a horse and carriage. As a result, he decided that he would make the streets as safe as he could. He came up with a new type of traffic signal. Morgan's invention was a T-shaped pole that had three signals. The first signal was stop, the second signal was go, and the third signal stopped traffic all ways. It made all the cars, carts, and horses stop for a few seconds. Then it changed to go for some of the traffic. That made it safer for drivers. It also allowed people to cross busy streets safely. He received a patent for the signal in 1923.

The amount of traffic we have now is greater than it was in Morgan's time. However, we can still see his type of signal making the streets safe. He would probably be proud of his invention if he saw how it worked today.

GO ON →

Now answer Numbers 6 through 10. Base your answers on "Stopping Traffic."

6 Read the sentences from the article.

During this time, <u>the streets of Cleveland were a circus</u>. It was common for bicycles, horse-pulled wagons, and cars to share the same streets.

What does "the streets of Cleveland were a circus" mean?

(A) The streets were very busy.

(B) Many animals traveled the streets.

(C) The streets were closed for a circus.

(D) Many people used the sidewalks.

7 How does the author connect Morgan's inventions of the gas mask and the T-shaped pole?

(A) by comparing the two inventions

(B) by describing the effect each invention had

(C) by listing the common steps in the creation of each invention

(D) by explaining the problems Morgan had with each invention

GO ON →

8 Read the sentences from the article.

Morgan's <u>mind was a whirlwind</u>. He was always thinking about what he could do next.

What does "mind was a whirlwind" mean?

(A) He made a quick motion.

(B) He had many ideas for inventions.

(C) He read many stories at once.

(D) He was always moving something.

9 What happened as a result of Morgan's invention of the traffic signal? Pick **two** choices.

(A) Driving vehicles became much safer.

(B) Car wrecks became more common.

(C) The amount of traffic on the streets increased greatly.

(D) People were able to cross busy streets safely.

(E) All the cars, carts, and horses had to move for a few seconds.

GO ON →

10 Draw a line to match **each** statement with an invention.

Morgan finds a way to make driving much safer.		Sewing Machine

| Morgan becomes an important person in Cleveland. | | Gas Mask |

| Morgan's invention is used by soldiers in the U.S. Army. | | Traffic Signal |

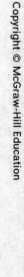

STOP

Name: _____ Date: _____

Now answer Number 11. Base your answer on "Helping Each Other" and "Stopping Traffic."

11 Use text evidence to explain how barn raisings and Morgan's traffic signal both helped to develop towns and cities.

_____

_____

_____

_____

_____

_____

_____

_____

_____

_____

_____

_____

_____

Answer Key

Question	Correct Answer	Content Focus	CCSS	Complexity
1A	D	Text Structure: Cause and Effect	RI.3.8	DOK 2
1B	see below	Text Structure: Cause and Effect/ Text Evidence	RI.3.8 RI.3.1	DOK 2
2	C	Figurative Language: Metaphors	L.3.5a	DOK 2
3	D	Text Structure: Cause and Effect	RI.3.8	DOK 2
4	A	Figurative Language: Metaphors	L.3.5a	DOK 2
5	D, E	Text Structure: Cause and Effect	RI.3.8	DOK 2
6	A	Figurative Language: Metaphors	L.3.5a	DOK 2
7	B	Text Structure: Cause and Effect	RI.3.8	DOK 2
8	B	Figurative Language: Metaphors	L.3.5a	DOK 2
9	A, D	Text Structure: Cause and Effect	RI.3.8	DOK 2
10	see below	Text Structure: Cause and Effect	RI.3.8	DOK 2
11	see below	Writing About Text	W.3.8	DOK 4

Comprehension 1A, 1B, 3, 5, 7, 9, 10	/12	%
Vocabulary 2, 4, 6, 8	/8	%
Total Weekly Assessment Score	/20	%

1B Students should underline the following sentences:
- First, people wanted to help those in need.
- If they could lend a hand, they would.
- Their help was a gift to their neighbor.

10 Students should complete the chart with the following statements:
- Sewing Machine- Morgan becomes an important person in Cleveland.
- Gas Mask- Morgan's invention is used by soldiers in the U.S. Army.
- Traffic Signal- Morgan finds a way to make driving much safer.

11 To receive full credit for the response, the following information should be included:
Barn raisings helped people develop a sense of community. When people left farms and moved to small towns, they used the same ideas for barn raisings to help make buildings for everyone to use. Morgan's traffic signal also helped because it made the town and city streets safe to drive on.

Read the article "Remembering the Soldiers" before answering Numbers 1 through 5.

Remembering the Soldiers

The Vietnam War began in the 1960s. It continued until 1973. Thousands of American soldiers fought in the war. Many of these soldiers died in Vietnam. Jan Scruggs was a soldier in Vietnam. He wanted people to remember the soldiers who had died in the war. He started the Vietnam Veterans Memorial Fund (VVMF) to raise money. The money would pay for a memorial. The memorial would honor the soldiers who had died in the war.

The VVMF decided to have a contest. The winner of the contest would design the memorial. More than 2,000 individuals and teams entered and became part of the contest. A student named Maya Lin won the contest. She was only 21 years old. She made a design of walls that listed the names of all the soldiers who died in the war. Maya Lin's design was simple but beautiful.

Work on the Vietnam Veterans Memorial started in March of 1982. The VVMF had raised more than eight million dollars by then. The walls were finished in November of 1982. The walls are made of a black stone called granite and are very shiny. They are almost like mirrors. The rest of the memorial included a statue of three soldiers and a flag. This was finished in 1984. The group decided to present the memorial to the American people that same year.

There are 58,272 names carved on the walls. They are the names of the soldiers who died in the war, and they come from every state. About 1,200 of the soldiers' names are listed as missing. The names are arranged by date. The first soldiers who died are the first names on the wall.

GO ON →

Eight of the names on the wall are women's names. Women did not fight in the Vietnam War. They worked mostly as nurses, but they served an important role in the war. In 1993 another statue was added to the memorial showing some of the women who served in the war.

There are trees and grass around the walls. The area is peaceful and quiet. People who visit the memorial are very moved by it. Many visitors are relatives of the soldiers who have died. Some are still very heartbroken. They find their relative's name on the wall. Seeing their relative's name helps them remember the soldier. Sometimes they make a rubbing of the name. They put a piece of paper over the name. Then they rub charcoal or crayon over it. The image of the name appears on the paper.

Visiting the Vietnam Veterans Memorial is a way to remember the soldiers who died in the war. The memorial is a beautiful and peaceful place. It is a place to honor the soldiers who fought for our country.

GO ON →

Now answer Numbers 1 through 5. Base your answers on "Remembering the Soldiers."

1 This question has two parts. First, answer part A. Then, answer part B.

Part A: What is the main idea of the article?

(A) Maya Lin created a beautiful design for the Vietnam Veterans Memorial.

(B) The memorial is a good way to remember all the soldiers who died in the war.

(C) The VVMF was started by Jan Scruggs, a soldier in Vietnam.

(D) Women played an important role in the war.

Part B: Which sentence **best** explains the main idea of the article?

(A) "Maya Lin's design was simple but beautiful."

(B) "The VVMF had raised more than eight million dollars by then."

(C) "The memorial would honor the soldiers who had died in the war."

(D) "The rest of the memorial included a statue of three soldiers and a flag."

GO ON →

2 Read the sentence from the article.

People who visit the memorial are very <u>moved</u> by it.

Which sentence uses the word <u>moved</u> in the same way it is used above?

(A) Martin moved his chair closer.

(B) The music moved Ms. Wu to tears.

(C) Carmen moved from Houston to Dallas.

(D) The dancers moved gracefully across the floor.

3 Which paragraph would **best** be supported by the following detail?

The women were important to the war effort, too.

(A) paragraph 4, page 49

(B) paragraph 1, page 50

(C) paragraph 2, page 50

(D) paragraph 3, page 50

GO ON →

4 This question has two parts. First, answer part A. Then, answer part B.

Part A: Read the sentence from the article.

The group decided to <u>present</u> the memorial to the American people that same year.

Which meaning of the word <u>present</u> is the same one used in the sentence above?

Ⓐ give

Ⓑ play

Ⓒ sing

Ⓓ write

Part B: Which sentence uses the word <u>present</u> in the same way it is used in the sentence in Part A?

Ⓐ Danny received the best present for his birthday.

Ⓑ Anna cannot not finish her homework at the present time.

Ⓒ The students wanted to present their teacher with an award.

Ⓓ Fred had to be present for his exam.

5 The Vietnam Veterans Memorial is a way to remember the soldiers who died in the war. Pick **three** details from the article that **best** support this idea.

Ⓐ The walls of the memorial have the names of the soldiers who died.

Ⓑ The Vietnam War started in the 1960s.

Ⓒ More than 2,000 individuals entered the contest.

Ⓓ People are very moved when they visit the memorial.

Ⓔ Seeing their relative's name helps them honor the soldier.

Ⓕ The shiny walls are made of a black stone called granite.

GO ON →

Read the article "The River of Grass" before answering Numbers 6 through 10.

The River of Grass

Over the flat land of southern Florida lie ponds, marshes, and forests. Together, they form the Everglades. People used to call the Everglades "the river of grass." Water flowed through the sawgrass marshes. This made the marshes look like a river of grass.

At one time, the Everglades covered nearly 11,000 square miles. The land was home to hundreds of different kinds of animals. Rare birds made their home there. Alligators and crocodiles lived together. Unusual flowers and trees grew in the warm, damp area.

The state of Florida began to drain and take away some of the water from the Everglades. This allowed farmers to grow crops. Large farms and then cities sprang up. The draining went on as canals and dams moved water out of the Everglades into the ocean. The river of grass was no longer a river.

The Everglades changed. Animals that had lived there for hundreds of years were now in danger. Plants that had once grown there could not live. New plants took over. Salty water moved into the marshes. Many of the alligators died.

In the 1920s, the public started to object to draining the Everglades. People began to see that the Everglades was an amazing place. Many people wanted to help save the area. The leader of the National Park Service said the Everglades should be made a national park. This did not happen until 1947, though.

GO ON →

Threats to the Everglades continued. People built roads and buildings near the park. They took water that flowed into the park to use in other ways. By the year 2000, the Everglades was half the size it had been a hundred years before! The Everglades was in a lot of trouble.

In 2000, Florida and the national government worked out a plan. The plan will take more than 30 years to finish. The plan is to catch the fresh water that now flows into the ocean and bring the water back to the Everglades. Florida has other ideas too. The state plans to clean up Lake Okeechobee. Much of the Everglades' water comes from the lake. Florida will also work to get rid of new plants that have taken the place of the plants that used to grow there.

If Florida's plan is a success, the river of grass will flow again. The water of the Everglades will be clean. The plan will keep the rare plants and animals there. The Everglades will be a treasure for everyone. And the Everglades National Park will stay a place of wonder.

GO ON →

Now answer Numbers 6 through 10. Base your answers on "The River of Grass."

6 Read the sentence from the article.

The <u>land</u> was home to hundreds of different kinds of animals.

Which meaning of the word <u>land</u> is the same one used in the sentence above?

(A) arrive

(B) catch

(C) earth

(D) rest

7 This question has two parts. First, answer part A. Then, answer part B.

Part A: Read the sentence from the article.

In the 1920s, the public started to <u>object</u> to draining the Everglades.

Which sentence uses the word <u>object</u> in the same way it is used above?

(A) Paul placed the object carefully on the table.

(B) The mayor said he will object to the new plan.

(C) The puppy was an object of great interest to the class.

(D) Karim's object was to raise money for the playground.

Part B: Which meaning of the word <u>object</u> is the same one used in the sentence in Part A?

(A) to disagree

(B) a goal or plan

(C) to focus

(D) a thing to be used

GO ON →

8 This question has two parts. First, answer part A. Then, answer part B.

Part A: What is the main idea of the article?

Ⓐ The state of Florida drained water from the Everglades.

Ⓑ The Everglades needs help to remain a place of wonder.

Ⓒ The Everglades is home to many unusual plants and animals.

Ⓓ People wanted the Everglades to become a national park.

Part B: Which sentence **best** supports your answer in part A?

Ⓐ "Unusual flowers and trees grew in the warm, damp area."

Ⓑ "The leader of the National Park Service said the Everglades should be made a national park."

Ⓒ "The state of Florida began to drain and take away some of the water from the Everglades."

Ⓓ "Many people wanted to help save the area."

9 Which paragraph would **best** be supported by the following detail?

There is a plan to bring the water back to the Everglades.

Ⓐ paragraph 5, page 54

Ⓑ paragraph 1, page 55

Ⓒ paragraph 2, page 55

Ⓓ paragraph 3, page 55

GO ON →

10 What are some ideas the government came up with to save the Everglades? Pick **two** choices.

(A) build roads and buildings near the park

(B) clean up Lake Okeechobee

(C) take water that flowed into the park to use in other ways

(D) get rid of new plants that took the place of older plants

(E) use the Everglades for large farms and cities

Name: _____ Date: _____

Now answer Number 11. Base your answer on "Remembering the Soldiers" and "The River of Grass."

11 Explain why the Vietnam Veterans Memorial was built and why the Everglades became a national park. How did everyday people play a role in both? Support your answer with clear text evidence from both article.

_____

_____

_____

_____

_____

_____

_____

_____

_____

_____

_____

_____

_____

Answer Key

Name: _____

Question	Correct Answer	Content Focus	CCSS	Complexity
1A	B	Main Idea and Key Details	RI.3.2	DOK 2
1B	C	Main Idea and Key Details/ Text Evidence	RI.3.2 RI.3.1	DOK 2
2	B	Multiple-Meaning Words	L.3.4a	DOK 2
3	B	Main Idea and Key Details	RI.3.2	DOK 2
4	A	Multiple-Meaning Words	L.3.4a	DOK 2
5	A, D, E	Main Idea and Key Details	RI.3.2	DOK 2
6	C	Multiple-Meaning Words	L.3.4a	DOK 2
7	B	Multiple-Meaning Words	L.3.4a	DOK 2
8A	B	Main Idea and Key Details	RI.3.2	DOK 2
8B	D	Main Idea and Key Details/ Text Evidence	RI.3.2 RI.3.1	DOK 2
9	C	Main Idea and Key Details	RI.3.2	DOK 2
10	B, D	Main Idea and Key Details	RI.3.2	DOK 2
11	see below	Writing About Text	W.3.8	DOK 3

Comprehension 1A, 1B, 3, 5, 8A, 8B, 9, 10	/12	%
Vocabulary 2, 4, 6, 7	/8	%
Total Weekly Assessment Score	/20	%

11 To receive full credit for the response, the following information should be included: The Vietnam Veterans Memorial was built because a soldier wanted people to remember those who fought and died in the Vietnam War. The Everglades became a national park because people wanted to protect the plants and animals that lived in a part of Florida. Both the memorial and the park are here today because everyday people worked to make the memorial and the park happen.

Read the passage "The Thanksgiving Play" before answering Numbers 1 through 5.

The Thanksgiving Play

Mrs. Cook was concerned about the Thanksgiving play. Her third-grade class was not excited about the play rehearsals. Then on Monday, Julie announced that she no longer wanted to participate in the play. Everyone stopped and looked at her in surprise.

"I don't want to play the role of the mother," Julie said crossly. "The only part I play is to stir the pot and tell everyone to enjoy their meal."

"You have a very important role," Mrs. Cook said. "You're responsible for preparing and serving an incredible feast."

"I don't want to be a Pilgrim!" Mark said. "Why can't I have a more exciting part in the play?" He placed his hands on his hips in disgust. Then he shook his head angrily and stomped away.

Everyone started to complain loudly at the same time about the play. Even Fran had a scowl on her face. She was usually the happiest person in class. Mrs. Cook covered her ears and tried to get her class to cooperate. "Children, we have a play to perform," she said firmly. "We have to work together."

"Why do we have to do this play?" Lana asked. "Everyone's heard the Thanksgiving story a million times."

GO ON →

"Thanksgiving is the time to show gratitude for all we have," Mrs. Cook answered.

"Let's write a new play with a different setting," Tariq said. "We can play characters in the present time and write our own lines. Each one of us will explain what we are thankful for. I am going to write that I am thankful for snowy days."

"That's a fantastic idea!" shouted Karen. "I will give thanks for my brother."

"I think Tariq has proposed a wonderful idea. We all like it," said Mrs. Cook. "Let's start writing our lines for our play!"

"Can we still have our feast?" asked Mark. "Don't forget that it is an important part of the holiday, too."

All the children laughed. Now they were excited. So they immediately got busy planning and writing their play. Everyone wrote what they were thankful for and happily practiced their lines. They also worked together designing the stage for the play.

At last, Wednesday arrived. The children set up the stage. Then they stood behind the curtains and waited for the play to begin.

"Are you nervous?" Mrs. Cook asked. The children shook their heads and agreed they all were very calm.

"We aren't scared at all," Lana said. "The audience will be our friends and family. We want to tell them all what we are thankful for."

Mrs. Cook smiled. "I know they will enjoy your play," she said. "You did a terrific job working together." Then Mrs. Cook looked at her watch. "Everyone take your places! It's time for the play to begin." The auditorium grew dark. Then, the curtain slowly rose. All the children were smiling from ear to ear as the play began.

GO ON →

Now answer Numbers 1 through 5. Base your answers on "The Thanksgiving Play."

1 Read the sentences from the passage.

Everyone started to complain loudly at the same time about the play. Even Fran had a <u>scowl</u> on her face.

Which word means the **opposite** of <u>scowl</u>?

(A) frown

(B) grin

(C) scratch

(D) spot

2 Underline **two** sentences that belong in a summary of the story.

> ## Summary of "The Thanksgiving Play"
>
> The children do not want to do the Thanksgiving play.
>
> Tariq wants to tell everyone that he is thankful for snowy days.
>
> Mark decides he does not want to be a pilgrim in the play.
>
> The children work together and put on their own play.

GO ON →

3 This question has two parts. First, answer part A. Then, answer part B.

Part A: Read the sentence from the passage.

"That's a <u>fantastic</u> idea!" shouted Karen.

What does the word <u>fantastic</u> mean?

(A) favorite

(B) scary

(C) surprising

(D) wonderful

Part B: Which word means the **opposite** of <u>fantastic</u>?

(A) awful

(B) different

(C) gentle

(D) simple

4 This question has two parts. First, answer part A. Then, answer part B.

Part A: Which sentence **best** describes the lesson of the passage?

- Ⓐ You cannot please everybody.
- Ⓑ Be thankful for what you have.
- Ⓒ There is always someone worse off than you.
- Ⓓ A problem can be solved when people work together.

Part B: Which sentence **best** supports this idea?

- Ⓐ The children do not want to do the Thanksgiving play.
- Ⓑ The children laugh when Mark asks if they can have a feast.
- Ⓒ The children are happy when they write a new play together.
- Ⓓ The children stand on the stage and wait for the play to begin.

5 Which sentences **best** support the story's lesson? Pick **two** choices.

- Ⓐ "'I don't want to be a Pilgrim!' Mark said."
- Ⓑ "'Why can't I have a more exciting part in the play?'"
- Ⓒ "'Everyone's heard the Thanksgiving story a million times.'"
- Ⓓ "They also worked together designing the stage for the play."
- Ⓔ "The children shook their heads and agreed they all were very calm."
- Ⓕ "'You did a terrific job working together.'"

GO ON →

Read the passage "The Biggest Turnip" before answering Numbers 6 through 10.

The Biggest Turnip

Every spring, a farmer and his wife planted their garden. They planted peas, corn, beans, and tomatoes. They also planted turnips because they were the farmer's favorite. He liked the green leafy stem of the turnip. But he loved the big round root that grew underground.

All the vegetables grew beautifully. The farmer and his wife picked the peas, corn, beans, and tomatoes. Then they went to the part of the garden where the turnips were planted.

One turnip top stood apart. The green, leafy stem grew taller than the rest.

"This must be a pretty big turnip," the farmer said to his wife. "This will be delicious in our turnip soup!"

The farmer took hold of the turnip stem. He tried to pull the plant out of the ground. But the turnip below was too big and heavy. It would not come up. The farmer's wife put her arms around the farmer as he pulled, and she pulled, too. But they were too weak. The turnip would not come up.

The farmer's son came out to help. He pulled on his mother, who pulled on his father. But the turnip stayed in the ground. Then the farmer's daughter ran out to the garden. She pulled on her brother. He pulled on his mother, who pulled on the farmer. But the turnip would not move.

Two neighbors passed by.

"We can't do this alone. Please help us!" called the farmer's wife.

GO ON →

The neighbors joined the line, and everybody pulled. But they could not help remove the turnip either.

One of the neighbors ran to town and brought back the mayor, the baker, the tailor, the shoemaker, and a teacher. The line of people pulling was really long now. Still, they were not strong enough.

A stranger walked by. "What on Earth is going on here?" he asked.

"Please help us pull up our turnip," the farmer said.

And the stranger took his place at the end of the line, but still the turnip did not budge.

Then a little girl who was bouncing a ball and watching decided to join the line. She pulled on the stranger, who pulled on the teacher. The teacher pulled on the shoemaker, who pulled on the tailor. The tailor pulled on the baker, who pulled on the mayor. The mayor pulled on the neighbors. They all pulled as hard as they could. Suddenly, up came the turnip, and down everyone fell into a heap!

"Look at the size of that turnip!" everyone exclaimed.

The townspeople built a big fire outside the farmer's house. They set a gigantic kettle on top of the fire. Together they peeled the enormous turnip, cut it up, and put it in the kettle. When the soup was ready, they sat wherever they could to eat a bowlful.

The farmer said, "It took every single one of us, but we did it! We made the most delicious turnip soup ever!"

GO ON →

Now answer Numbers 6 through 10. Base your answers on "The Biggest Turnip."

6 Read the sentences from the story.

One turnip top stood <u>apart</u>. The green, leafy stem grew taller than the rest.

Which word has the **opposite** meaning of the word <u>apart</u> as used in the sentences above?

(A) away

(B) between

(C) together

(D) under

7 Put the events of the story in the correct sequence by numbering them from 1 to 4. Write the correct number in front of each event.

_____ | The farmer's son comes to help pull up the turnip. |

_____ | A little girl decides to help and joins the line pulling up the turnip. |

_____ | A stranger takes his place at the end of the line to help pull up the turnip. |

_____ | The neighbors join the line to help pull up the turnip. |

GO ON →

8 Choose **two** sentences that belong in a summary of the story.

(A) A farmer grows a very large turnip.

(B) The farmer's favorite vegetable is the turnip.

(C) A farmer and his wife grow many vegetables.

(D) A girl is bouncing a ball and watching everyone else.

(E) The whole town works together to pull up the turnip.

(F) A stranger asks the group of people why they are pulling.

9 This question has two parts. First, answer part A. Then, answer part B.

Part A: Read the sentences from the passage.

The townspeople built a big fire outside the farmer's house. They set a gigantic kettle on top of the fire.

What does the word gigantic mean?

(A) very old

(B) very large

(C) very smooth

(D) very delicate

Part B: Which word has the **opposite** meaning of the word gigantic?

(A) curved

(B) deep

(C) heavy

(D) tiny

GO ON →

10 This question has two parts. First, answer part A. Then, answer part B.

Part A: Which sentence **best** describes the lesson of the passage?

Ⓐ Good neighbors build good neighborhoods.

Ⓑ Eating healthy leads to a happy living.

Ⓒ Working together solves problems.

Ⓓ Never be too proud to ask for help.

Part B: Which sentence from the passage **best** supports your answer in part A?

Ⓐ "'This will be delicious in our turnip soup!'"

Ⓑ "'What on Earth is going on here?' he asked."

Ⓒ "'Look at the size of that turnip!' everyone exclaimed."

Ⓓ "The farmer said, 'It took every single one of us, but we did it!'"

Name: _____ Date: _____

Now answer Number 11. Base your answer on "The Thanksgiving Play" and "The Biggest Turnip."

11 How do the characters in the stories work together to solve their problems? Include information from both stories to support your answer.

_____

_____

_____

_____

_____

_____

_____

_____

_____

_____

_____

_____

Answer Key

Question	Correct Answer	Content Focus	CCSS	Complexity
1	B	Antonyms	L.3.4a	DOK 2
2	see below	Theme/Summary	RL.3.2	DOK 2
3A	D	Antonyms	L.3.4a	DOK 2
3B	A	Antonyms/Text Evidence	L.3.4a/ RL.3.1	DOK 2
4A	D	Theme	RL.3.2	DOK 3
4B	C	Theme/Text Evidence	RL.3.2/ RL.3.1	DOK 3
5	D, F	Theme	RL.3.2	DOK 3
6	C	Antonyms	L.3.4a	DOK 2
7	see below	Character, Setting, Plot: Sequence	RL.3.3	DOK 1
8	A, E	Theme/Summary	RL.3.2	DOK 2
9A	B	Antonyms	L.3.4a	DOK 2
9B	D	Antonyms/Text Evidence	L.3.4a/ RL.3.1	DOK 2
10A	C	Theme	RL.3.2	DOK 3
10B	D	Theme/Text Evidence	RL.3.2/ RL.3.1	DOK 3
11	see below	Writing About Text	W.3.8	DOK 4

Comprehension 2, 4A, 4B, 5, 7, 8, 10A, 10B		/12	%
Vocabulary 1, 3A, 3B, 6, 9A, 9B		/8	%
Total Weekly Assessment Score		/20	%

2 Students should underline the following sentences:
  • The children do not want to do the Thanksgiving play.
  • The children work together and put on their own play.

7 Students should number the events as follows:
  • 1 - The farmer's son comes to help pull up the turnip.
  • 2 - The neighbors join the line to help pull up the turnip.
  • 3 - A stranger takes his place at the end of the line to help pull up the turnip.
  • 4 - A little girl decides to help and joins the line pulling up the turnip.

11 To receive full credit for the response, the following information should be included:
The students in the story, "The Thanksgiving Play" do not want to put on the play of the Thanksgiving story. The students agree to work together to put on their own play. They plan and write their own Thanksgiving play. In the story, "The Biggest Turnip" a farmer and his wife cannot pull up a huge turnip from their garden. Many of the townspeople help the farmer and his family pull up the huge turnip.

Read the passage "Going Away" before answering Numbers 1 through 5.

Going Away

Janek stood by the gate as he waited for his grandpa to find the ticket and passport. The airport was as busy as an anthill with people hurrying this way and that. It was Janek's first time in an airport. He was feeling nervous and scared. Never before had he been on a plane. It would take many hours to fly from Poland to the United States. Grandpa would not be coming with him. How quickly life had changed!

"I don't want to leave you!" cried Janek. "Look at this airport! I will get lost without you. That is what will happen to me in California, too."

Janek hated being at the airport, and everyone here seemed unhappy. All around him were mothers with babies that screamed like fire truck sirens. People were rushing around with worried faces. Janek thought of the brown cows on the farm back home and the white chickens that scratched the earth. This morning, Janek had eaten his last egg from those chickens. He had enjoyed his last pear from the old tree in the yard. Now he was going to a new place. Everything in his life would be different.

"Janek," Grandpa said gently, "your life in California will be very much like your life here. The children play soccer there just as they do here, and they like to read books just like you. You will make many new friends. Your father now has a job and an apartment. He is thrilled that you will be with him again. Besides, he misses you very much."

Then the loud speaker clicked on. The sharp sound made Janek jump like a scared rabbit. A woman's voice said it was time to board the plane. Grandpa squeezed Janek tightly and said, "When you are unhappy, look in this envelope. Now go ahead and get on the plane."

GO ON →

Janek said, "I will miss you, Grandpa!" Then he took the envelope and walked to the plane. Janek's legs shook like jelly as he went through the door alone. Soon the plane lifted off the ground and flew up high into the dark sky. Janek glanced out the window. He saw one star that sparkled like a diamond ring. He opened the envelope and wiped away a tear that slipped down his cheek. Inside was a photograph of Grandpa smiling! His hat was pushed back on his head. There was his old wood house, too. Janek smiled. He would write a letter to Grandpa as soon as he arrived at his new home.

GO ON →

Name: _____ Date: _____

Now answer Numbers 1 through 5. Base your answers on "Going Away."

1 Read the sentence from the passage.

<u>The airport was as busy as an anthill</u> with people hurrying this way and that.

What does "the airport was as busy as an anthill" mean?

Ⓐ The airport was very active.

Ⓑ There were anthills near the airport.

Ⓒ The people were running away from ants.

Ⓓ The airport was built to look like an anthill.

2 Which details belong in a summary of the passage? Choose **two** sentences from the box below and write them in the chart.

Summary of "Going Away"

Sentences:
Janek hugs his grandpa goodbye.
Everyone seems unhappy at the airport.
Janek is nervous because he is flying for the first time.
The loudspeaker announces it is time to get on the plane.
Janek is leaving the home he knows to live with his father.

GO ON →

3 Read the sentence from the passage.

Janek's legs shook like jelly as he went through the door alone.

What does "Janek's legs shook like jelly" mean?

(A) He spilled jelly on his legs and feet.

(B) He was scared and his legs were weak.

(C) He was hungry because he did not eat breakfast.

(D) He had trouble walking because the floor was shaking.

4 Which words **best** describe how Janek feels when he sees Grandpa's picture? Pick **two** choices.

(A) angry

(B) comforted

(C) confused

(D) happy

(E) silly

(F) worried

GO ON →

Name: _____ Date: _____

5 This question has two parts. First, answer part A. Then, answer part B.

Part A: What is the lesson of this story?

(A) It is important to give your best effort.

(B) Believe in yourself, even when others do not.

(C) Do not worry about what others think about you.

(D) Change can be scary, but it brings new opportunities.

Part B: Which sentence from the passage **best** supports the story's lesson?

(A) "'Look at this airport!'"

(B) "'You will make many new friends.'"

(C) "'Besides, he misses you very much.'"

(D) "'Now go ahead and get on the plane.'"

GO ON →

Read the passage "The Pepper Palace" before answering Numbers 6 through 10.

The Pepper Palace

"Hector and Rosa," Grandma Maria said, "take the brooms and go sweep the sidewalk outside the restaurant. I want it as neat as a pin out there." Rosa frowned and replied, "Grandma, I want to go play with Lori."

"Why do I always have to do chores at the restaurant?" asked Hector. "I hate this old restaurant!"

"Why, Hector and Rosa Santana!" Grandma Maria said, shocked. "The Pepper Palace is the most important thing in our family! This restaurant is the heart of the Santana family. Have I ever told you how it started?"

"No, Grandma," Rosa said, her brown eyes as big as saucers. "Please tell us!" Grandma Maria, Rosa, and Hector sat at one of the empty tables in the restaurant. Grandma Maria told the story of her own grandparents, Luisa and Juan.

Luisa and Juan lived in a small village in Mexico. Juan was a wonderful gardener. He grew tomatoes as red as the setting sun. His chili peppers were hot, hot, hot. His bell peppers were as sweet as honey, and his corn grew tall and golden. Luisa was a marvelous cook. She always used Juan's beautiful vegetables. Everyone in town loved to eat their food.

"We should go to the United States," Luisa said to Juan. "We can work hard and open a restaurant there. It would be our very own business. It would be a dream come true."

GO ON →

Luisa and Juan had to wait many months before they could come to this country. Juan had an aunt who lived in Texas. When the time finally came, they went to live with her. Juan worked at gardening, the job he loved. Luisa cooked for people's parties and special events. After several years, they were able to open their own restaurant, this restaurant, the Pepper Palace.

The Pepper Palace was very popular right from the start. People came from far away, as hungry as bears waking from their long winter nap. They came hungry, but after eating the dishes Luisa cooked with Juan's vegetables, they left happy and full. When Luisa and Juan had children, they helped in the restaurant. Their son Carlos took over the cooking. When Carlos had children, his oldest daughterMaria became the cook.

"And that is me," said Grandma Maria. "You see, this restaurant was my grandparents' dream. They came to this country and worked to make their dream come true. Now Texas is our home."

"Wow," said Hector. "Maybe when I grow up, I can cook at the Pepper Palace!"

"No, I want to be the cook!" Rosa protested.

Grandma Maria laughed. "You can both cook," she promised. "You can both carry on our family's dream."

GO ON →

Now answer Numbers 6 through 10. Base your answers on "The Pepper Palace."

6 Read the sentences from the story.

"No, Grandma," Rosa said, her brown eyes <u>as big as saucers</u>. "Please tell us!"

Why does the author say that Rosa's eyes are "as big as saucers"?

Ⓐ to show that they sparkle

Ⓑ to show that they look brown

Ⓒ to show how pretty Rosa looks

Ⓓ to show how surprised Rosa looks

7 This question has two parts. First, answer part A. Then, answer part B.

Part A: What is the lesson of this story?

Ⓐ Grandmothers can be very wise.

Ⓑ Family is more important than work.

Ⓒ Dreams can come true with hard work.

Ⓓ Brothers and sisters should work together.

Part B: Which detail from the passage **best** supports the story's lesson?

Ⓐ Juan and Luisa worked hard to open their restaurant.

Ⓑ Hector and Rosa do not want to sweep the sidewalk.

Ⓒ Luisa and Juan lived in a small village in Mexico.

Ⓓ Rosa is upset that she cannot play with Lori.

GO ON →

8 Read the sentence from the story.

People came from far away, <u>as hungry as bears</u> waking from their long winter nap.

What does the author suggest with the phrase "as hungry as bears"?

(A) The people wanted the food at the restaurant.

(B) The people seemed scary to Luisa and Juan.

(C) The people were large and could eat a lot.

(D) The people were loud and in a bad mood.

9 Which sentence **best** states the theme of the story? Underline the sentence below.

"And that is me," said Grandma Maria. "You see, this restaurant was my grandparents' dream. They came to this country and worked to make their dream come true. Now Texas is our home."

"Wow," said Hector. "Maybe when I grow up, I can cook at the Pepper Palace!"

"No, I want to be the cook!" Rosa protested.

GO ON →

10 How do Hector and Rosa feel about the restaurant after their grandma tells them the story about how it started? Pick **two** choices.

(A) They do not want to do chores.

(B) They are very proud of their family.

(C) They want to help at the restaurant.

(D) They do not want to play outside anymore.

(E) They are excited to open their own restaurant.

(F) They are worried that the restaurant will close.

Name: _____ Date: _____

Now answer Number 11. Base your answer on "Going Away" and "The Pepper Palace."

11 What do the lessons from "Going Away" and "The Pepper Palace" tell you about why people move to a new country? Include information from both stories to support your answer.

_____

_____

_____

_____

_____

_____

_____

_____

_____

_____

_____

_____

Answer Key

Question	Correct Answer	Content Focus	CCSS	Complexity
1	A	Figurative Language: Similes	RL.3.4	DOK 2
2	see below	Theme/Summary	RL.3.2	DOK 2
3	B	Figurative Language: Similes	RL.3.4	DOK 2
4	B, D	Character, Setting, Plot: Character	RL.3.3	DOK 2
5A	D	Theme	RL.3.2	DOK 3
5B	B	Theme/Text Evidence	RL.3.2/ RL.3.1	DOK 3
6	D	Figurative Language: Similes	RL.3.4	DOK 2
7A	C	Theme	RL.3.2	DOK 3
7B	A	Theme/Text Evidence	RL.3.2/ RL.3.1	DOK 3
8	A	Figurative Language: Similes	RL.3.4	DOK 2
9	see below	Theme	RL.3.2	DOK 3
10	B, C	Theme	RL.3.2	DOK 2
11	see below	Writing About Text	W.3.8	DOK 4

Comprehension 2, 4, 5A, 5B, 7A, 7B, 9, 10	/12	%
Vocabulary 1, 3, 6, 8	/8	%
Total Weekly Assessment Score	/20	%

2 Students should write the following sentences in the chart:
- Janek is nervous because he is flying for the first time.
- Janek is leaving the home he knows to live with his father.

9 Students should underline the following sentence:
- They came to this country and worked to make their dream come true.

11 To receive full credit for the response, the following information should be included: In "Going Away," Janek does not want to leave his grandfather but moves to California to start a new life with his father. In "The Pepper Palace," Luisa and Juan move to Texas to make their dream of owning a restaurant come true. In both stories, the characters move to another country to make a better life for themselves.

Read the article "Voting" before answering Numbers 1 through 5.

Voting

In Mr. Jensen's third-grade classroom, the students are standing in a circle having a discussion. What should their classroom pet be? Students in the class disagree in answering this question.

Some students want a hamster. Trish explains why. "A hamster is as quiet as a mouse. It's easy to take care of. Plus, it will teach us about mammals. We can learn about how mammals live. We can see what they eat. We can watch when they sleep."

Other students dislike that idea. They give another answer. They prefer a snake for a classroom pet. Jonah says, "A snake is more interesting and unusual. It is long and slides across the ground. A snake will teach us about reptiles. We can learn what makes reptiles different from other animals."

The students are unable to agree on what kind of pet they want. Mr. Jensen asks the students to be reseated so they can take a vote.

The students who want a hamster raise their hands. Mr. Jensen walks around the classroom counting them. To be sure, he recounts their hands. Then he writes the number of votes on the board. He does the same for those students who want a snake.

Which pet do you think wins?

Sometimes it is difficult for a group of people to agree on one decision. Voting is the best way to decide issues. Voting offers people choices. By having the chance to vote, people decide which choice they like best. The choice that receives the most votes wins. The winning choice tells what most of the people in the group think.

GO ON →

Just as the students voted in the classroom, people in our country vote. They have the chance to vote for people to serve in our government. Voting is one of our greatest rights as American citizens. Through voting, citizens decide who they want to run the government. They vote for people who will represent them and state their views. Citizens also help decide what actions the government should take. Voting is one way that citizens make their voices heard. They choose between the people running for president. The winner becomes president for four years. He or she leads the entire country. Voters also choose between people to represent them in Congress. This is where laws are made for the entire country.

Voting can help groups make decisions, just like it helped the students in Mr. Jensen's class choose a pet. The students raised their hands. They selected which animal they wanted as their classroom pet.

So which animal won the most votes in Mr. Jensen's classroom? It was the snake!

GO ON →

Name: _____ Date: _____

Now answer Numbers 1 through 5. Base your answers on "Voting."

1 This question has two parts. First, answer part A. Then, answer part B.

Part A: Read the sentence from the article.

Jonah says, "A snake is more interesting and <u>unusual</u>."

If *usual* means "common," what does <u>unusual</u> mean?

Ⓐ not common

Ⓑ being common

Ⓒ acting common

Ⓓ equally common

Part B: What is the meaning of the prefix *un-* in <u>unusual</u>?

Ⓐ again

Ⓑ before

Ⓒ the same as

Ⓓ the opposite of

2 Complete the chart by writing the main idea and the supporting details in the correct boxes. Use all of the sentences.

Main Idea:
Detail:
Detail:
Detail:

Sentences:

Voters choose who will be president.

Voting is an important right for U.S. citizens.

People vote for others who will state their views.

Citizens vote to decide who will run the government.

3 Read the sentence from the article.

To be sure, he <u>recounts</u> their hands.

What does the word <u>recounts</u> mean?

(A) does not count

(B) counts wrong

(C) counts before

(D) counts again

GO ON →

4 This question has two parts. First, answer part A. Then, answer part B.

Part A: What is the author's point of view about voting?

Ⓐ It is fair to almost everyone.

Ⓑ It is done in every country.

Ⓒ It is difficult to understand.

Ⓓ It is not used to solve problems.

Part B: Which sentence from the article **best** supports your answer in part A?

Ⓐ "Mr. Jensen walks around the classroom counting them."

Ⓑ "Sometimes it is difficult for a group of people to agree on one decision."

Ⓒ "The winning choice tells what most of the people in the group think."

Ⓓ "Voting is one way that citizens make their voices heard."

5 With which ideas would the author **most likely** agree? Pick **two** choices.

Ⓐ Voters have a say in our government.

Ⓑ Voting does not offer us many choices.

Ⓒ Not all citizens should be allowed to vote.

Ⓓ Voting does not take place often in the U.S.

Ⓔ Citizens should vote when they are given the opportunity.

Ⓕ Some people think voting is more important than it really is.

GO ON →

Read the article "Saving a Grassland" before answering Numbers 6 through 10.

Saving a Grassland

Otero Mesa is a special place. No other area in the country is quite like it. It stretches as far as the eye can see. Tall grasses sway in the breeze. Desert plants send their flower spikes up toward the sky. It is too dry for trees.

A variety of wildlife calls this grassy land home. Prairie dogs dig their tunnels and dens under the grass. Mule deer and antelope graze on it. Songbirds and eagles fly in the blue skies above it.

Beneath, Otero is special, too. Huge amounts of fresh water lie below the ground.

People have used and lived on this grassland for centuries. Ancient Native American ruins dot the mesa. Some pictures carved on rocks are more than one thousand years old.

Several years ago, the government suggested a plan. It would allow drilling and mining on the grassland. Many people were unhappy with the plan. They were afraid that the plants and animals would be harmed. Hikers, hunters, and ranchers wanted to keep using and enjoying the grassland. Scientists wanted to study its wildlife, rocks, and water. The Apache wanted to protect the ruins of their ancestors.

Many of these people started working together. They wrote letters and e-mails to the government in Washington, D.C. They called their government representatives to ask them to stop the plan. They signed petitions. A petition is a written request signed by many people that asks the government to do something. Americans have the right to petition their government. It is an important right.

GO ON →

This is how our government works. Voters choose people to send to Washington, D.C. These people represent the voters. But they need to know what voters think. They do not want to misunderstand voters' wishes. If they do, they might make laws that voters do not want. People must let the government know what they want.

After many months, a court ruled against the drilling plan. The court told the government to rethink the plan. It said the government must consider the effects on nature before it allowed drilling.

The people who worked against the plan were happy. For now, the people have reclaimed this land as a wilderness area. No one can drill on it. No one can mine on it. But the future of Otero Mesa is still uncertain. So, many of these determined people are working together again. They want the government to call the land a wilderness area. That means the animals and plants would be protected. The land could not be used except for recreation. Once again, these people are writing letters and e-mails. They are calling their representatives. They are signing petitions. They want to make sure drilling and mining are never allowed on the Otero Mesa.

GO ON →

Name: _____ Date: _____

Now answer Numbers 6 through 10. Base your answers on "Saving a Grassland."

6 Read the sentence from the article.

Many people were <u>unhappy</u> with the plan.

What does the word <u>unhappy</u> mean?

Ⓐ happy before

Ⓑ happy again

Ⓒ very happy

Ⓓ not happy

7 This question has two parts. First, answer part A. Then, answer part B.

Part A: What is the author's point of view about Otero Mesa?

Ⓐ It is an important part of history.

Ⓑ It is a very special and different place.

Ⓒ There are too many animals living in it.

Ⓓ There is a lot that people don't know about it.

Part B: Which sentence from the article **best** summarizes the author's point of view?

Ⓐ "No other area in the country is quite like it."

Ⓑ "Tall grasses sway in the breeze."

Ⓒ "A variety of wildlife calls this grassy land home."

Ⓓ "Mule deer and antelope graze on it."

GO ON →

8 This question has two parts. First, answer part A. Then, answer part B.

Part A: Read the sentence from the article.

For now, the people have <u>reclaimed</u> this land as a wilderness area.

What does the word <u>reclaimed</u> mean?

(A) The people had it before.

(B) The people want to take it.

(C) The people will give it back.

(D) The people have taken it again.

Part B: What is the meaning of the prefix *re-* in <u>reclaimed</u>?

(A) again

(B) before

(C) the same as

(D) the opposite of

9 Which **two** sentences show the author's point of view in the article?

(A) "It is too dry for trees."

(B) "Prairie dogs dig their tunnels and dens under the grass."

(C) "Beneath, Otero is special, too."

(D) "Several years ago, the government suggested a plan."

(E) "It is an important right."

(F) "Voters choose people to send to Washington, D.C."

GO ON →

Name: _____ Date: _____

10 With which statements would the author agree? Choose **two** statements below and write them in the chart.

Author's Point of View	

Statements:

Otero Mesa is not a protected place.

The government should protect nature.

People should be allowed to drill on natural land.

The government is too busy to listen to our concerns.

Americans should let the government know what they think.

Name: _____ Date: _____

Now answer Number 11. Base your answer on "Voting" and "Saving a Grassland."

11 How do the authors' points of view in the articles help readers understand how to voice their opinion? Include information from both articles to support your answer.

_____

_____

_____

_____

_____

_____

_____

_____

_____

_____

_____

_____

_____

_____

Answer Key

Question	Correct Answer	Content Focus	CCSS	Complexity
1A	A	Prefixes: *un-*	L.3.4b	DOK 1
1B	D	Prefixes: *un-*/Text Evidence	L.3.4b/ RI.3.1	DOK 1
2	see below	Main Idea and Key Details	RI.3.2	DOK 2
3	D	Prefixes: *re-*	L.3.4b	DOK 1
4A	A	Author's Point of View	RI.3.6	DOK 3
4B	C	Author's Point of View/ Text Evidence	RI.3.6/ RI.3.1	DOK 3
5	A, E	Author's Point of View	RI.3.6	DOK 3
6	D	Prefixes: *un-*	L.3.4b	DOK 1
7A	B	Author's Point of View	RI.3.6	DOK 3
7B	A	Author's Point of View/ Text Evidence	RI.3.6/ RI.3.1	DOK 3
8A	D	Prefixes: *re-*	L.3.4b	DOK 1
8B	A	Prefixes: *re-*/Text Evidence	L.3.4b/ RI.3.1	DOK 1
9	C, E	Author's Point of View	RI.3.6	DOK 3
10	see below	Author's Point of View	RI.3.6	DOK 3
11	see below	Writing About Text	W.3.8	DOK 4

Comprehension 2, 4A, 4B, 5, 7A, 7B, 9, 10	/12	%
Vocabulary 1A, 1B, 3, 6, 8A, 8B	/8	%
Total Weekly Assessment Score	/20	%

2 Students should complete the chart with the following sentences:
- Main Idea: Voting is an important right for U.S. citizens.
- Details: Voters choose who will be president; People vote for others who will state their views; Citizens vote to decide who will run the government.

10 Students should complete the chart with the following statements:
- The government should protect nature.
- Americans should let the government know what they think.

11 To receive full credit for the response, the following information should be included:
In the article "Voting," the author believes voting is the best way to decide issues and offers people choices. In the article "Saving a Grassland," the author believes Americans have the right to petition their government when they do not agree with it.

Read the article "A Bee-Friendly Garden" before answering Numbers 1 through 5.

A Bee-Friendly Garden

Our lives would be different without bees. Bees help plants grow. Many plants produce the fruits and vegetables we eat. Without bees, these fruits and vegetables could not grow. Bees are truly wonderful creatures.

Yet the number of bees is now low. It is getting even lower. Scientists are unsure why. Some people are fearful for their future. They think that bees may die off. We must do something about this problem. One solution is to make our gardens bee-friendly.

One of the most careless things to do is spray insect killer. Insect killer does work. It kills the insects that eat plants. But it can also be harmful to bees. Some insect killers can kill the bee before it returns to the hive. Others can get carried back by bees. This could harm the rest of the hive. Insect pests can be stopped in other ways. For example, ladybugs and praying mantises eat pests. Wiping insect soap on plants leaves can also kill pests. These two methods do not harm bees.

Making our gardens bee-friendly can also add to the bee population. Planting a bee garden is a great idea. Bee gardens provide nectar and pollen for the bees. A successful bee garden would have flowers that bloom over the spring, summer, and fall. The flowers need to be planted in bunches of like flowers. The garden would also have different types of plants that are closely grouped together.

GO ON →

Many people believe that all bees live in hives. That is untrue. Some bees dig into the ground. There, they build their nests. They lay their eggs. When people lay wood chips or other materials on the ground, bees cannot dig nests. So here is another good way to help bees. When you are working outside, leave loose dirt in flower beds and gardens.

Some bees nest in old pieces of wood. Others nest in holes. Still others nest in buildings or trees. Gardens can be made to provide spaces like these for bees. Trees or walls that block wind are a good idea. So are shady areas. These help bees to escape the hot sun. Trees and overhangs can protect bees from hard rains. Bee gardens also provide bees with water. Bees need water just like people do.

Making a bee-friendly garden is far from a useless task. The rewards are worth the effort. A bee-friendly garden is beautiful and colorful. Most importantly, it keeps bees healthy and happy.

GO ON →

Name: _____ Date: _____

Now answer Numbers 1 through 5. Base your answers on "A Bee-Friendly Garden."

1 This question has two parts. First, answer part A. Then, answer part B.

Part A: Read the sentence from the article.

Some people are <u>fearful</u> for their future.

What does the word <u>fearful</u> mean?

Ⓐ being very afraid

Ⓑ being without fear

Ⓒ being afraid over and over again

Ⓓ being afraid before there is danger

Part B: What is the meaning of the suffix *-ful* in <u>fearful</u>?

Ⓐ again

Ⓑ before

Ⓒ full of

Ⓓ having none

GO ON →

2 Read the sentence from the article.

One of the most <u>careless</u> things to do is spray insect killer.

What does the word <u>careless</u> mean?

(A) paying attention again

(B) paying much attention

(C) before paying attention

(D) without paying attention

3 Underline the sentence in the paragraph that **best** summarizes the author's point of view about bee gardens.

Making our gardens bee-friendly can also add to the bee population. Planting a bee garden is a great idea. Bee gardens provide nectar and pollen for the bees. A successful bee garden would have flowers that bloom over the spring, summer, and fall. The flowers need to be planted in bunches of like flowers. The garden would also have different types of plants that are closely grouped together.

GO ON →

4 This question has two parts. First, answer part A. Then, answer part B.

Part A: What is the author's point of view about bees?

(A) They are important to our world.

(B) They are necessary for other insects.

(C) They do not belong in flower gardens.

(D) They do not help us as much as they could.

Part B: Which sentence from the article **best** summarizes the author's point of view about bees?

(A) "Our lives would be different without bees."

(B) "Bees help plants grow."

(C) "Yet the number of bees is now low."

(D) "Insect killer does work."

5 With which sentences would the author of the article **most likely** agree? Pick **two** choices.

(A) Wood chips should cover the ground of a bee garden.

(B) The dirt in bee gardens should not be loose.

(C) Bee gardens should have many flowers.

(D) Bees do not need water like people do.

(E) Planting a bee garden is not helpful.

(F) It is important to help bees survive.

GO ON →

Read the article "The Manatee" before answering Numbers 6 through 10.

The Manatee

It is not pretty to look at. It is not as friendly as a dolphin. It does not sing like a whale. But the manatee is beautiful in its own way. It has special qualities all its own. The manatee is a rare animal that needs our help.

The manatee is a large mammal. It can grow up to 13 feet long. That is about the length of a car. It can weigh more than 1,000 pounds! The manatee swims in warm, shallow waters. It is found along the coast and inland waterways of Florida. In the summer, manatees may swim as far west as Texas.

Even though the manatee is huge, it is one of the most graceful swimmers. It glides through the water. The manatee uses its powerful tail to propel it. It steers with its fins. Even though it is big, the manatee is a gentle animal. It munches on sea grasses and other water plants. Its size and peaceful nature give it the nickname "sea cow."

The manatee has a wrinkled gray body. It looks hairless. But like all mammals, it does have hair. Also, like all mammals, manatees have lungs to breathe air. The manatee will come to the surface of the water to breathe. Sometimes people will see its nose sticking out of the water.

This can be a problem for manatees. It is dangerous for them to be near the surface of the water when motorboats race by. The blades of boat propellers can cut them when they come up to breathe. Many manatees have scars from these cuts. Others are killed when boats hit them.

GO ON →

People also cause other problems for manatees. The animals sometimes get trapped in canal locks and floodgates that people have built. Others get caught in crab nets. Then they cannot come up to breathe. Some manatees swallow fishhooks and fishing lines. These items are harmful to the animals. Removing these items when they have been swallowed by the animal is dangerous. Because of these actions by people, manatees are now endangered. That means the number of manatees has become so low that they may die out.

Everyone should be concerned about manatees. There are many people that are misinformed. Everyone should help save them. The government has correctly made the manatee a protected animal. That means it is a crime to harm one. Boaters must not be so careless. They should follow speed limits where manatees live. People should learn more about this amazing creature. They should learn how to protect it. Then this gentle giant will continue to live on without these threats.

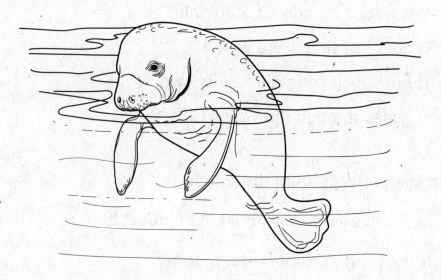

GO ON →

Name: _____ Date: _____

Now answer Numbers 6 through 10. Base your answers on "The Manatee."

6 This question has two parts. First, answer part A. Then, answer part B.

Part A: What is the author's point of view about the manatee?

Ⓐ It is hard to watch while it swims.

Ⓑ It is pretty when it is not moving.

Ⓒ It is beautiful on the inside.

Ⓓ It is very heavy-looking.

Part B: Which sentence from the article **best** summarizes the author's point of view?

Ⓐ "It is not as friendly as a dolphin."

Ⓑ "It does not sing like a whale."

Ⓒ "It has special qualities all its own."

Ⓓ "It glides through the water."

7 Read the sentence from the article.

The manatee uses its <u>powerful</u> tail to propel it.

What does the word <u>powerful</u> mean?

Ⓐ weak

Ⓑ strong

Ⓒ in need of power

Ⓓ having power again

GO ON →

8 Read the sentence from the article.

It looks <u>hairless</u>.

What does the word <u>hairless</u> explain?

(A) The manatee looks like it needs hair.

(B) The manatee looks like it has no hair.

(C) The manatee looks like it has a lot of hair.

(D) The manatee looks like it used to have hair.

9 How are the ideas connected in the fifth and sixth paragraphs of the article? Pick **two** choices.

(A) They explain why manatees are endangered.

(B) They explain why people love manatees so much.

(C) They describe how manatees get caught in fishing nets.

(D) They describe problems that people cause for manatees.

(E) They explain why manatees need to come up for air to breathe.

(F) They describe how manatees are being protected by the government.

GO ON →

10 Circle **two** ideas that the author would **most likely** agree with, based on evidence from the text.

> ## Author's Point of View
>
> Manatees cause many problems for people.
>
> Everyone should be concerned about the manatees.
>
> Boaters are not a real danger to manatees.
>
> People should work to protect manatees.
>
> Whales are more important than manatees.

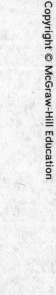

Name: _____ Date: _____

Now answer Number 11. Base your answer on "A Bee-Friendly Garden" and "The Manatee."

11 How are the points of view of the authors **alike**? Include information from both articles to support your answer.

_____

_____

_____

_____

_____

_____

_____

_____

_____

_____

_____

_____

_____

Name: _____

Question	Correct Answer	Content Focus	CCSS	Complexity
1A	A	Suffixes: *-ful*	L.3.4b	DOK 1
1B	C	Suffixes: *-ful*/Text Evidence	L.3.4b/ RI.3.1	DOK 1
2	D	Suffixes: *-less*	L.3.4b	DOK 1
3	see below	Author's Point of View	RI.3.6	DOK 3
4A	A	Author's Point of View	RI.3.6	DOK 3
4B	A	Author's Point of View/ Text Evidence	RI.3.6/ RI.3.1	DOK 3
5	C, F	Author's Point of View	RI.3.6	DOK 3
6A	C	Author's Point of View	RI.3.6	DOK 3
6B	C	Author's Point of View/ Text Evidence	RI.3.6/ RI.3.1	DOK 3
7	B	Suffixes: *-ful*	L.3.4b	DOK 1
8	B	Suffixes: *-less*	L.3.4b	DOK 1
9	A, D	Text Structure: Cause and Effect	RI.3.8	DOK 2
10	see below	Author's Point of View	RI.3.6	DOK 3
11	see below	Writing About Text	W.3.8	DOK 4

Comprehension 3, 4A, 4B, 5, 6A, 6B, 9, 10	/12	%
Vocabulary 1A, 1B, 2, 7, 8	/8	%
Total Weekly Assessment Score	/20	%

3 Students should underline the following sentence in the paragraph:
- Planting a bee garden is a great idea.

10 Students should circle the following sentences:
- Everyone should be concerned about the manatees.
- People should work to protect manatees.

11 To receive full credit for the response, students should include that both authors favor protecting the insect and mammal whose survival is at risk and why the student feels it is important to protect them.

**Read the poem "Number Dance" before answering
Numbers 1 through 5.**

Number Dance

I know that I can add well—
That two plus four is six.
But when I try to multiply,
My mind starts playing tricks.

The numbers all escape me
Like fireflies at night
And even if I try my best,
I still can't do it right!

I multiply by one just fine,
But then I try by two.
My brain is like a scrambled egg—
It's just so hard to do!

Now, two times two is four, I think.
But what is two times three?
The answer slips away just like
A squirrel runs up a tree.

The numbers all start whirling
Like dancers on a stage.
They jump and spin and won't stay put.
They leap right off the page!

GO ON →

"Practice, Mark," my teacher says.
"It's really just the same
As if you were a pitcher
Preparing for a game."

I get my team together—
Miguel, Nick, Jane, and me.
We start with two times two and then
Go on to two times three.

We've got the threes and fours done.
We've learned six, seven, eight—
Team Number's going down now,
Team Kid is doing great!

We practice hard together
And memorize them all,
Until at last I multiply
As well as I play ball.

GO ON →

Name: _____ Date: _____

Now answer Numbers 1 through 5. Base your answers on "Number Dance."

1 This question has two parts. First, answer part A. Then, answer part B.

Part A: Who is the speaker in the poem?

Ⓐ Jane

Ⓑ Mark

Ⓒ Miguel

Ⓓ Nick

Part B: Which lines from the poem show who the speaker is? Pick **two** choices.

Ⓐ "I know that I can add well—"

Ⓑ "My mind starts playing tricks."

Ⓒ "'Practice, Mark,' my teacher says."

Ⓓ "I get my team together—"

Ⓔ "Miguel, Nick, Jane, and me."

Ⓕ "Team Kid is doing great!"

GO ON →

2 Read the lines from the poem.

My brain is like a scrambled egg—
It's just so hard to do!

Why is the speaker's brain compared to a scrambled egg?

(A) to show how much the speaker likes eggs

(B) to explain how mixed-up the speaker feels

(C) to compare the differences of a brain and eggs

(D) to explain how hard it is to make scrambled eggs

3 Read the lines from the poem.

"It's really just the same
As if you were a pitcher
Preparing for a game."

Why does the teacher compare multiplying to preparing for a baseball game?

(A) to show that multiplication is used a lot in baseball

(B) to show that multiplying is harder than playing baseball

(C) to show that both multiplying and pitching take practice

(D) to show that all baseball pitchers are good at multiplying

GO ON →

4 Sort the words into the chart to show what the speaker thinks of multiplying at the beginning and end of the poem. Write each word in the correct place in the chart.

Beginning	End

Confusing	Easy	Hard	Helpful

5 With which statements would the speaker **most likely** agree? Pick **two** choices.

(A) Teachers can help students understand math.

(B) Multiplying confuses everyone.

(C) Practicing can help you multiply well.

(D) Multiplying is more fun than baseball.

(E) Baseball players always have to multiply.

(F) Practicing math makes your mind play tricks.

GO ON →

Read the poem "Science Night" before answering Numbers 6 through 10.

Science Night

It's almost time for Science Night.
I need a partner. Who should I ask?
I have three friends who all want to help.
How can I choose just one for the task?

My best friend Jule is fun to be around
But she's as chatty as a bird.
When she starts to talk – well, just watch out!
I can't get in a single word.

Still, that might work for Science Night;
She'd show our project to the crowd.
Jule's voice would boom out like a drum.
I wouldn't mind if she were extra loud!

And then there's Dan, who's really shy
But wise as an owl—he's so smart!
He'd help with the thinking for the job.
He wouldn't talk, but he'd do his part.

GO ON →

But what about Shel, who's good at art?
He paints and draws and sculpts so well.
Our project would look great—no doubt!
I'm sure I should be asking Shel.

How can I choose just one from three?
I need them all! I'm feeling sick.
I'm as dizzy as a spinning top.
When trying to choose, I just can't pick!

But wait—why not ask them all to help?
A group of four is better than one.
I'd love to work with all my friends.
In such a group, we'd have such fun!

The work could be shared by four of us
By me and Shel and Dan and Jule.
We'd fit together like puzzle pieces
And take the grand prize in the school!

GO ON →

Name: _____ Date: _____

Now answer Numbers 6 through 10. Base your answers on "Science Night."

6 This question has two parts. First, answer part A. Then, answer part B.

Part A: Who is the speaker in the poem?

(A) a judge at a school science night

(B) a science teacher assigning science projects

(C) a student who does not like science projects

(D) a student who needs to choose a partner for a project

Part B: Which line from the poem **best** shows who the speaker is?

(A) "It's almost time for Science Night."

(B) "I need a partner. Who should I ask?"

(C) "I have three friends who all want to help."

(D) "How can I choose just one for the task?"

7 Read the line from the poem.

Jule's voice would boom out like a drum.

Why is Jule's voice compared to a drum?

(A) to show that Jule plays drums

(B) to show how loud Jule's voice is

(C) to show how much the speaker likes drums

(D) to show that Jule's voice makes many sounds

GO ON →

8 Draw lines to show the speaker's point of view of each friend in the poem.

Jule	very smart

Dan	a great artist

Shel	likes to talk

9 Read the lines from the poem.

The work could be shared by four of us
By me and Shel and Dan and Jule.
We'd fit together like puzzle pieces
And take the grand prize in the school!

Why does the speaker say they will "fit together like puzzle pieces"?

(A) to show how well they will all work together

(B) to show how difficult their science project is

(C) to show how their science project is a puzzle

(D) to show how good they are at doing puzzles

GO ON →

10 Choose **two** things that the speaker learns in the poem.

(A) Everyone has a talent.

(B) Projects should be done alone.

(C) Puzzles are easy to put together.

(D) Friends can make a project better.

(E) Science is not as hard as it may seem.

(F) It is difficult to decide on a project topic.

Name: _____ Date: _____

Now answer Number 11. Base your answer on "Number Dance" and "Science Night."

11 The speakers in these poems have strong feelings about a problem they are each facing. Use text evidence to show each speaker's point of view and how the speaker solves the problem.

_____

_____

_____

_____

_____

_____

_____

_____

_____

_____

_____

_____

_____

_____

Answer Key

Name: _____

Question	Correct Answer	Content Focus	CCSS	Complexity
1A	B	Point of View	RL.3.6	DOK 3
1B	C, E	Point of View/Text Evidence	RL.3.6/ RL.3.1	DOK 3
2	B	Figurative Language: Similes	L.3.5a	DOK 2
3	C	Figurative Language: Similes	L.3.5a	DOK 2
4	see below	Point of View	RL.3.6	DOK 3
5	A, C	Point of View	RL.3.6	DOK 3
6A	D	Point of View	RL.3.6	DOK 3
6B	B	Point of View/Text Evidence	RL.3.6/ RL.3.1	DOK 3
7	B	Figurative Language: Similes	L.3.5a	DOK 2
8	see below	Point of View	RL.3.6	DOK 2
9	A	Figurative Language: Similes	L.3.5a	DOK 2
10	A, D	Theme	RL.3.2	DOK 3
11	see below	Writing About Text	W.3.8	DOK 4

Comprehension 1A, 1B, 4, 5, 6A, 6B, 8, 10		/12	%
Vocabulary 2, 3, 7, 9		/8	%
Total Weekly Assessment Score		/20	%

4 Students should complete the chart as follows:
- Team Number: Confusing, Hard
- Team Kid: Successful, Helpful

8 Students should make the following matches:
- Jule—likes to talk
- Dan—very smart
- Shel—a great artist

11 To receive full credit for the response, the following information should be included:
Mark has trouble remembering his multiplication facts. The other speaker has trouble choosing a partner for a science project. Mark learns multiplication by using baseball and his friends as examples to figure out math. The other speaker solves her problem by working on the science project with all of her friends instead of just one.

Read the passage "The Hare and the Well" before answering Numbers 1 through 5.

The Hare and the Well

Long ago, in a village in Africa, the animals were worried. It had not rained for many weeks and the land was as dry as dust. The animals were thirsty. They needed water. Lion, who was king of the animals, called them all together. Elephant, Baboon, Hyena, Tortoise, Antelope, Hare, Giraffe, and Buffalo all came. They decided to dig a well. Everyone agreed, except Hare. He wanted nothing to do with the work of digging.

For several days, the animals worked very hard. Elephant dug with his trunk. Baboon, Hyena, and Giraffe dug with their front paws. Tortoise, Antelope, and Buffalo hauled the dirt away on their backs. Hare sat in the shade beneath a palm tree, laughing at them. Finally, the animals struck water in the ground. Cool, clean water seeped into the well.

King Lion ruled that all the animals would share the water, except for Hare. But Hare paid no attention to that law. He would creep down the side of the well and take great big gulps of water. So the animals decided to place a guard by the well. Elephant said he would be first.

That evening, Hare approached Elephant with a big jar. "Would you like some sweet honey?" he asked.

"Why yes," Elephant nodded. So Hare gave him a lick of honey from the jar. While Elephant was enjoying the taste, Hare rubbed honey on Elephant's front legs and then on his back legs. Then he scurried in a figure-8 around Elephant until Elephant got all twisted up and his legs stuck together. He couldn't move. Hare scampered down the well. He drank all the water he desired and ran away.

GO ON →

The next night, Antelope replaced Elephant as guard, but Hare tricked Antelope as well. Each night, a different animal guarded the well. Each night, Hare tricked an animal and got his water. And each night, King Lion became more and more furious.

Finally, it was Tortoise's turn. He had his own idea of how to guard the water. Instead of sitting beside the well, Tortoise crawled down into it. When Hare came to the well that night, he saw no guard. Hare laughed. "They've given up!" he said aloud. "They know they can't keep me out of the well."

With that, Hare dived into the well. He landed right on Tortoise's hard shell. THUD!

Hare was a bit dazed. Tortoise carried him out of the well and straight to King Lion. The king punished Hare harshly. Hare was most sorry. He promised never to steal water again.

And from that day on, the animals enjoyed clean, cool water from their well.

GO ON →

Now answer Numbers 1 through 5. Base your answers on "The Hare and the Well."

1 What is the **main** problem in the passage?

(A) The well is very hard to dig.

(B) It has rained very little for weeks.

(C) Elephant's legs are stuck together.

(D) Hare keeps taking water from the well.

2 Read the sentences from the passage.

Each night, Hare tricked an animal and got his water. And each night, King Lion became more and more <u>furious</u>.

Which word has almost the **same** meaning as <u>furious</u>?

(A) afraid

(B) angry

(C) ashamed

(D) awful

GO ON →

3 This question has two parts. First, answer part A. Then, answer part B.

Part A: How do the animals solve their problem?

Ⓐ Tortoise crawls into the well.

Ⓑ Elephant guards the well all day.

Ⓒ They fill the well with water each day.

Ⓓ They dig the well deeper to get more water.

Part B: Which sentence from the passage **best** shows how the problem is solved?

Ⓐ "That evening, Hare approached Elephant with a big jar."

Ⓑ "Each night, a different animal guarded the well."

Ⓒ "When Hare came to the well that night, he saw no guard."

Ⓓ "Tortoise carried him out of the well and straight to King Lion."

GO ON →

4 What happens when King Lion punishes Hare? Pick **two** choices.

    Ⓐ Hare tricks Antelope.

    Ⓑ Hare falls into the well.

    Ⓒ The animals can enjoy the water.

    Ⓓ The animals dig a well to get water.

    Ⓔ The animals place a guard by the well.

    Ⓕ Hare promises never to steal water again.

5 Draw a line to match each underlined word in the sentences on the left with the word that has the **same** meaning on the right.

Tortoise, Antelope, and Buffalo <u>hauled</u> the dirt away on their backs.	hurried
Hare <u>scampered</u> down the well.	carried
He drank all the water he <u>desired</u> and ran away.	wanted

GO ON →

Read the passage "The Lion and the Mouse" before answering Numbers 6 through 10.

The Lion and the Mouse

A Retelling of Aesop's Fable

One day a great lion was dozing in the forest. A tiny gray mouse came scurrying along. In a hurry to get home, she didn't take the time to run around the lion. Instead, she ran up the lion's tail, over his back, through his mane, and down his nose. By that time, the lion had awakened. He opened one eye. When the mouse leapt off the lion's nose onto the ground, the lion took a mighty swipe with his paw. It landed on the mouse's tail, stopping her in her tracks.

"How dare you crawl on the King of Beasts!" the lion roared.

The mouse was terrified that the lion would crush her. She squeaked, "Oh please, great lion. I was in a hurry to get home. I did not mean any harm. I did not intend to wake you."

"But wake me you did!" the lion replied. "And now with my powerful paw, I will—"

"Wait!" pleaded the mouse. "If you set me free, one day I will repay you. I will help you, I promise."

"Hah!" the lion laughed. "How can a mouse as tiny as an ant ever help a great beast like me?"

But the lion was so amused by the idea that he decided to let the mouse go. She scampered away into the forest.

GO ON →

Many days later, three hunters entered the forest. They were seeking to bring back a lion for a zoo. Creeping along, they saw the mighty lion napping once again. They threw a large rope net over him and tied it to a tree. The lion twisted and turned and pulled against the net with all his strength, but it did not help. He could not break the ropes. He roared his loudest roar, but the hunters were not frightened. They smiled and left to get a cart to carry the lion off. The King of the Beasts had been captured!

Far away, the little mouse heard the lion's roar and came scurrying. "Oh my," she cried when she saw the lion trapped in the rope net. Then, without hesitating, she immediately began to chew through the net. She used her sharp teeth to gnaw away at first one rope and then another. Soon the lion was freed from the snare.

The lion lifted the mouse gently up on his paw. "If it were not for you, I would no longer be King of the Beasts," he said softly. "You were right, little one. Even a creature as tiny as you can help a mighty animal like me."

GO ON →

Now answer Numbers 6 through 10. Base your answers on "The Lion and the Mouse."

6 This question has two parts. First, answer part A. Then, answer part B.

Part A: Read the paragraph from the passage.

The mouse was <u>terrified</u> that the lion would crush her. She squeaked, "Oh please, great lion. I was in a hurry to get home. I did not mean any harm. I did not intend to wake you."

What does the word <u>terrified</u> mean in the paragraph?

(A) very scared

(B) very bold

(C) very mad

(D) very sure

Part B: Which word has almost the **same** meaning as <u>terrified</u>?

(A) angry

(B) brave

(C) certain

(D) frightened

GO ON →

7 How does the mouse get the lion to let her go after he catches her? Pick **two** things that she does.

(A) She makes the lion laugh.

(B) She helps the lion fall asleep.

(C) She promises to trick the hunters.

(D) She helps the lion practice his roar.

(E) She promises to repay the lion one day.

(F) She makes the lion feel bad about catching her.

8 This question has two parts. First, answer part A. Then, answer part B.

Part A: What is the **main** problem in the passage?

(A) The lion is in the mouse's way.

(B) The lion is caught in a hunting net.

(C) The mouse needs to hurry to get home.

(D) The hunters need a cart to carry the lion.

Part B: How is the problem solved?

(A) The mouse calls for help.

(B) The hunters set the lion free.

(C) The lion uses his sharp claws.

(D) The mouse helps the lion get free.

GO ON →

9 Read the sentence from the passage.

Then, without <u>hesitating</u>, she immediately began to chew through the net.

Which word means almost the **same** as <u>hesitating</u>?

(A) biting

(B) pausing

(C) realizing

(D) speaking

10 Underline the sentence below that **best** states the theme of the passage.

The lion lifted the mouse gently up on his paw. "If it were not for you, I would no longer be King of the Beasts," he said softly. "You were right, little one. Even a creature as tiny as you can help a mighty animal like me."

Now answer Number 11. Base your answer on "The Hare and the Well" and "The Lion and the Mouse."

11 In both passages, the characters have a problem. How do they solve their problems in similar ways? Include information from both passages to support your answer.

_____

_____

_____

_____

_____

_____

_____

_____

_____

_____

_____

_____

_____

Answer Key

Name: _____

Question	Correct Answer	Content Focus	CCSS	Complexity
1	D	Character, Setting, Plot: Problem and Solution	RL.3.3	DOK 2
2	B	Synonyms	L.3.4a	DOK 2
3A	A	Character, Setting, Plot: Problem and Solution	RL.3.3	DOK 2
3B	D	Character, Setting, Plot: Problem and Solution/Text Evidence	RL.3.3/ RL.3.1	DOK 2
4	C, F	Character, Setting, Plot: Problem and Solution	RL.3.3	DOK 2
5	see below	Synonyms	L.3.4a	DOK 2
6A	A	Synonyms	L.3.4a	DOK 2
6B	D	Synonyms/Text Evidence	L.3.4a/ RL.3.1	DOK 2
7	A, E	Character, Setting, Plot: Problem and Solution	RL.3.3	DOK 2
8A	B	Character, Setting, Plot: Problem and Solution	RL.3.3	DOK 2
8B	D	Character, Setting, Plot: Problem and Solution/Text Evidence	RL.3.3/ RL.3.1	DOK 2
9	B	Synonyms	L.3.4a	DOK 2
10	see below	Theme	RL.3.2	DOK 3
11	see below	Writing About Text	W.3.8	DOK 4

Comprehension 1, 3A, 3B, 4, 7, 8A, 8B, 10		/12	%
Vocabulary 2, 5, 6A, 6B, 9		/8	%
Total Weekly Assessment Score		/20	%

5 Students should match the following synonyms:
- hauled—carried
- scampered—hurried
- desired—wanted

10 Students should underline the following sentence:
- "Even a creature as tiny as you can help a mighty animal like me."

11 To receive full credit for the response, the following information should be included: In both passages, characters use a special quality to solve their problem. Tortoise uses his hard shell to catch Hare and stop him from taking the water. The mouse uses her sharp teeth to chew through the net and free the lion.

Read the passage "Green Juice" before answering Numbers 1 through 5.

Green Juice

Every night, each member of the Willet family is expected to help with dinner. Tonight, Eddie decided to surprise everyone by making a juice they have never had before. He got out a pitcher and spoon. Just as he opened the refrigerator, his sister strolled into the kitchen.

"Are we having apple or orange juice tonight?" Marcy asked.

"Neither," answered Eddie. "I'm tired of drinking the same old boring juice. I've decided to surprise everyone. I'm making something different— green juice."

Marcy's mouth opened as wide as the Grand Canyon. She couldn't believe he was going through with this. Eddie did a lot of strange things, but this time he had gone too far.

"Now," Eddie told her. "All I have to do is follow an easy recipe that I found." Eddie showed Marcy a page that he had ripped from a recent issue of a cooking magazine. On the page was a photograph of a tall glass of bright green juice. "It will be a piece of cake to make this exciting new juice!" Eddie exclaimed.

"I don't like to try new things," Marcy grumbled. "I have absolutely no desire to drink green juice." Her stomach turned at the thought of drinking something that was green.

"How do you know it won't taste good?" Eddie asked.

"Juice should be orange, purple, or red," Marcy said. "It's definitely not supposed to be green!" He knew his sister might have to be coaxed into trying the new drink. "This will be something new," Eddie told her. "It's fun to try new things."

GO ON →

"Green juice is indeed new, but I don't think it will be fun to try!" Marcy exclaimed. Marcy decided that if Eddie was determined to do this, she was not going to stay there and watch him! She left the kitchen shaking her head at Eddie's bizarre idea. Just moments later, Marcy returned to the kitchen to set the table. She saw that Eddie had finished making his strange juice. It was very green. Marcy watched her brother as he poured some of the green liquid into a glass. She held her breath in disgust as Eddie took a drink.

"How does it taste?" she asked. Eddie smiled because he knew that Marcy was a bit curious.

"It's magnificent!" exclaimed Eddie. "I think it's the best juice I've ever made and would even call my creation a masterpiece. I am a juice artist!" He extended the glass in her direction and Marcy stared thoughtfully at the glass. Eddie was confident that Marcy would sample his exciting new drink.

"I certainly don't like the look of it, but I guess you can't judge a book by its cover!" Marcy said. Marcy wrinkled her nose and took the glass from Eddie. Then she cautiously took a tiny sip. "Wow! It tastes like apple juice and a bit like grape juice, too. I like it!" Marcy exclaimed. "I think you hit the nail on the head! What ingredients did you put in it to make it green and still give it this amazing flavor?"

"I have a secret ingredient," Eddie answered.

"What is it?" Marcy asked. "I can't tell you," said Eddie with a smile. "Then it wouldn't be a secret anymore."

GO ON →

Name: _____ Date: _____

Now answer Numbers 1 through 5. Base your answers on "Green Juice."

1 Which statements **best** explain why Eddie makes the green juice? Pick **two** choices.

Ⓐ He likes to do strange things.

Ⓑ He wants to make his sister nervous.

Ⓒ He wants to play a joke on his family.

Ⓓ He thinks his mother will like the juice.

Ⓔ He thinks it will taste better if it is green.

Ⓕ He is tired of drinking the same boring juice.

2 Read the sentence from the story.

Her stomach turned at the thought of drinking something that was green.

What does the phrase "her stomach turned" explain about Marcy?

Ⓐ She feels sick.

Ⓑ She feels angry.

Ⓒ She feels thirsty.

Ⓓ She feels hungry.

GO ON →

3 Complete the chart to show causes and effects in the passage. Write each statement below in the correct place in the chart.

Cause	→	Effect
Marcy does not like to try new things.	→	
	→	

Statements:

Eddie wants Marcy to drink the green juice.

Marcy does not want to try the green juice.

Eddie thinks it is fun to try new things.

4 Read the sentences from the passage.

"I like it!" Marcy exclaimed. "I think you hit the nail on the head!"

What does the phrase "hit the nail on the head" mean?

(A) Marcy thinks Eddie did something silly.

(B) Marcy thinks Eddie did something wrong.

(C) Marcy thinks Eddie did something just right.

(D) Marcy thinks Eddie did something with a tool.

GO ON →

5 This question has two parts. First, answer part A. Then, answer part B.

Part A: Why does Marcy drink the green juice after Eddie calls it his masterpiece?

Ⓐ She is curious about how it tastes.

Ⓑ She is tired of listening to him talk about it.

Ⓒ She is thirsty from helping her parents make dinner.

Ⓓ She is nervous he will be mad if she doesn't drink it.

Part B: Which sentence from the passage **best** supports your answer in part A?

Ⓐ "She held her breath in disgust as Eddie took a drink."

Ⓑ "'I think it's the best juice I've ever made and would even call my creation a masterpiece.'"

Ⓒ "He extended the glass in her direction and Marcy stared thoughtfully at the glass."

Ⓓ "'What ingredients did you put in it to make it green and still give it this amazing flavor?'"

GO ON →

Read the passage "Piñata Party" before answering Numbers 6 through 10.

Piñata Party

Nola was so excited. She had just received an invitation to her friend Elle's birthday party. Elle was going to be nine years old. Nola loved birthday parties. She loved eating cake and ice cream and singing "Happy Birthday!" Above all, she loved hitting the piñata and watching all the candy burst out.

"I'd love to come to your birthday party," Nola told Elle at school the next day. "What shape of piñata are you going to have?"

"Oh, we won't have a piñata," Elle replied.

"Why not?" Nola asked, surprised.

"My brother can't eat sugar," Elle replied. "So I don't like eating candy and things like that either. But we'll play lots of good games, and my mother makes great fruit treats." Nola hid her disappointment from Elle. But later that day, she talked with her friend Ami about it. "How can you have fun at a party without a piñata?" she asked. "How can you have a party without candy?"

Ami was folding paper into beautiful butterfly shapes. "Actually, I don't eat much candy myself," Ami replied. Then, after a pause, she looked up and said, "But who says a piñata has to be filled with candy? Why not fill it with — butterflies?"

"You mean your paper butterflies?" Nola asked. "What fun will that be?"

"It will be great fun!" Ami insisted. "The butterflies will all flutter though the air. And they'll be our paper butterflies because you're going to help me make them. Let's not let the cat out of the bag and make it a big surprise for everyone!"

GO ON →

Nola scrunched up her nose, but then she shrugged her shoulders and decided to go along with Ami's idea. For the next few hours, the girls were as busy as beavers. They cut and folded pretty pastel colors of tissue paper over and over. At first Nola was all thumbs. But as she carefully watched Ami's hands and practiced, her butterflies became as good as Ami's. Ami's mother lent a hand by making a large piñata in the shape of a butterfly. The girls stuffed all their butterflies inside before Ami's mother sealed it.

When the girls arrived at Elle's party, they presented her with the piñata. "Don't worry," Nola said. "There's no candy inside. There's a surprise."

The piñata was hung and all the kids took turns whacking at it until—FWOP!—the piñata burst. Dozens of paper butterflies fluttered down. The kids all squealed with delight.

Elle shouted, "Everyone try to catch as many as you can! Whoever catches the most will win a prize!"

"You were right," Nola giggled to Ami, as she snatched a butterfly that was landing on Ami's head. "This beats candy!"

GO ON →

Now answer Numbers 6 through 10. Base your answers on "Piñata Party."

6 Circle the paragraph in which Elle tells Nola why she will not have a piñata at her party.

"I'd love to come to your birthday party," Nola told Elle at school the next day. "What shape of piñata are you going to have?"

"Oh, we won't have a piñata," Elle replied.

"Why not?" Nola asked, surprised.

"My brother can't eat sugar," Elle replied. "So I don't like eating candy and things like that either. But we'll play lots of good games, and my mother makes great fruit treats." Nola hid her disappointment from Elle. But later that day, she talked with her friend Ami about it. "How can you have fun at a party without a piñata?" she asked. "How can you have a party without candy?"

GO ON →

7 This question has two parts. First, answer part A. Then, answer part B.

Part A: Read the sentence from the passage.

Let's not let <u>the cat out of the bag</u> and make it a big surprise for everyone!"

What does the phrase "let the cat out of the bag" mean as it is used in the sentence?

Ⓐ surprise a cat

Ⓑ give away a secret

Ⓒ keep a gift in a bag

Ⓓ play a trick on someone

Part B: Which word in the sentence is the **best** clue about what the phrase means?

Ⓐ make

Ⓑ big

Ⓒ surprise

Ⓓ everyone

8 Which sentences tell what happens when the piñata bursts? Pick **two** choices.

Ⓐ Candy falls out of the piñata.

Ⓑ Ami grabs all of the butterflies.

Ⓒ The kids all cheer in happiness.

Ⓓ The butterflies fall out of the piñata.

Ⓔ The butterflies do not fall out of the piñata.

Ⓕ Elle is surprised to find the piñata is empty.

GO ON →

9 Read the sentences from the passage.

At first Nola was <u>all thumbs</u>. But as she carefully watched Ami's hands and practiced, her butterflies became as good as Ami's.

What does the phrase "all thumbs" tell about Nola?

Ⓐ Her hands are very sore.

Ⓑ She is quick with her hands.

Ⓒ Her hands are very powerful.

Ⓓ She is clumsy with her hands.

10 This question has two parts. First, answer part A. Then, answer part B.

Part A: Which sentence **best** describes the lesson of the passage?

Ⓐ It can be fun to try new things.

Ⓑ Everyone should have a second chance.

Ⓒ Friends do not always agree on everything.

Ⓓ Treat others as you would like to be treated.

Part B: Which detail from the passage **best** supports your answer in part A?

Ⓐ The kids take turns hitting the piñata.

Ⓑ The girls give Elle the piñata at the party.

Ⓒ Nola tells Ami that the butterflies are much better than candy.

Ⓓ Elle tells everyone to try to catch as many butterflies as they can.

Name: _____ Date: _____

Now answer Number 11. Base your answer on "Green Juice" and "Piñata Party."

11 In both passages, Marcy and Nola change the way they feel about something. How do each of their feelings change? Include information from both passages to support your answer.

_____

_____

_____

_____

_____

_____

_____

_____

_____

_____

_____

_____

_____

_____

Answer Key

Name: _____

Question	Correct Answer	Content Focus	CCSS	Complexity
1	A, F	Character, Setting, Plot: Cause and Effect	RL.3.3	DOK 2
2	A	Figurative Language: Idioms	RL.3.4	DOK 2
3	see below	Character, Setting, Plot: Cause and Effect	RL.3.3	DOK 2
4	C	Figurative Language: Idioms	RL.3.4	DOK 2
5A	A	Character, Setting, Plot: Cause and Effect	RL.3.3	DOK 2
5B	C	Character, Setting, Plot: Cause and Effect/ Text Evidence	RL.3.3/ RL.3.1	DOK 2
6	see below	Character, Setting, Plot: Cause and Effect	RL.3.3	DOK 2
7A	B	Figurative Language: Idioms	RL.3.4	DOK 2
7B	C	Figurative Language: Idioms/Text Evidence	RL.3.4/ RL.3.1	DOK 2
8	C, D	Character, Setting, Plot: Cause and Effect	RL.3.3	DOK 2
9	D	Figurative Language: Idioms	RL.3.4	DOK 2
10A	A	Theme	RL.3.2	DOK 3
10B	C	Theme/Text Evidence	RL.3.2/ RL.3.1	DOK 3
11	see below	Writing About Text	W.3.8	DOK 4

Comprehension 1, 3, 5A, 5B, 6, 8, 10A, 10B		/12	%
Vocabulary 2, 4, 7A, 7B, 9		/8	%
Total Weekly Assessment Score		/20	%

3 Students should complete the chart as follows:
- Cause—Marcy does not like to try new things./Effect—Marcy does not want to try the green juice.
- Cause—Eddie thinks it is fun to try new things./Effect—Eddie wants Marcy to drink the green juice.

6 Students should circle the following paragraph:
- "My brother can't eat sugar," Elle replied. "So I don't like eating candy and things like that either. But we'll play lots of good games, and my mother makes great fruit treats."

11 To receive full credit for the response, the following information should be included: Marcy's point of view changes because she is curious about the green juice and decides to drink it. She likes the taste of the juice and learns that she should not judge something by the way it looks. Nola's view changes because she is willing to try a new way of preparing a piñata for a party. She learns that it can be just as fun to use paper butterflies as it is to use candy.

Read the article "Mysterious Mars" before answering Numbers 1 through 5.

Mysterious Mars

People have always been curious about Mars. After all, it is close to Earth and can be easily seen with a telescope. Moreover, Mars is much like Earth. It is a rocky planet that has valleys, hills, and plains. For years people wanted to know if there was life on Mars. So scientists started looking for facts. What have they found out?

Water is important for all living things. Without it, plants and animals cannot live. So scientists first searched for signs of water on Mars. They looked through a powerful telescope. They saw that the main areas of the planet looked like dry stream beds. Now most experts firmly believe that there was water on Mars long ago.

Scientists also know that Mars is very cold. The freezing temperatures would make it difficult to live there. Moreover, large dust storms sweep across the surface of the planet. They may last for many months. Sometimes dust covers the whole planet. It dims the sun's light. It would be hard for living things to breathe or see in such a dusty place.

GO ON →

NASA is a group of people that is responsible for space travel and research. They built spacecraft to visit Mars. The first spacecraft flew to Mars in 1975. Its name was *Viking*. One of its jobs was to look for signs of life. *Viking* took lots of photographs. The pictures showed proof that scientists were right—nothing could live on Mars.

NASA sent *Pathfinder* to Mars in 1996. It went to test rocks and soil. It gathered special details about the weather on Mars. *Pathfinder* sent more than 16,000 photographs back to Earth. Scientists looked closely at the pictures and information to discover more facts about the planet. They wondered if there was water under the ice caps. They also wanted to know if any plants or animals had ever lived there. Then in 1999, *Mars Polar Lander* traveled to Mars. Its job was to look for water under the planet's south ice cap. This space trip did not go well. Sadly, the spacecraft was lost before it was able to explore the area.

With the *Mars Polar Lander* gone, NASA had to go back to the drawing board. It ended up sending two robots to Mars in 2004. Their names are *Spirit* and *Opportunity*. The robots' mission was to move around the planet and take photographs. They also picked up soil and rocks. NASA tested the materials to see what they were made of. *Spirit* and *Opportunity* have collected lots of details about this mysterious planet. Scientists are still finding out new facts about Mars all the time. Perhaps someday, they will discover if there was ever life on the planet.

GO ON →

Now answer Numbers 1 through 5. Base your answers on "Mysterious Mars."

1 This question has two parts. First, answer part A. Then, answer part B.

Part A: Read the sentence from the article.

It is a <u>rocky</u> planet that has valleys, hills, and plains.

The suffix *-y* means "full of." What does the word <u>rocky</u> tell about Mars?

(A) It has many trees.

(B) It has many lakes.

(C) It has many stones.

(D) It has many streams.

Part B: Which word uses the suffix *-y* in the same way as <u>rocky</u>?

(A) any

(B) chunky

(C) factory

(D) toy

GO ON →

2 Complete the chart by writing the main idea of the article and the supporting details in the correct boxes. Use all of the sentences.

Main Idea	
Supporting Details	

Sentences:

Mars is similar to Earth in some ways.

NASA has had many missions to Mars.

Plants and animals cannot survive on Mars.

Scientists still have a lot to learn about Mars.

3 Read the sentence from the article.

Now most experts <u>firmly</u> believe that there was water on Mars long ago.

If you <u>firmly</u> believe something, how do you feel about it?

(A) angry

(B) certain

(C) confused

(D) happy

GO ON →

4 Read the paragraph from the article.

Scientists also know that Mars is very cold. The freezing temperatures would make it difficult to live there. Moreover, large dust storms sweep across the surface of the planet. They may last for many months. Sometimes dust covers the whole planet. It dims the sun's light. It would be hard for living things to breathe or see in such a dusty place.

Pick **two** main ideas that make up the paragraph.

(A) Dust makes life on Mars difficult.

(B) Scientists know that Mars is very cold.

(C) There are freezing temperatures on Mars.

(D) Dust storms on Mars can dim the sun's light.

(E) Dust storms on Mars can last for many months.

(F) Cold temperatures make it difficult to live on Mars.

5 This question has two parts. First, answer part A. Then, answer part B.

Part A: What is the **main** responsibility of NASA?

(A) to study rocks and soil from Mars

(B) to study the weather patterns on Mars

(C) to research and develop new spacecraft

(D) to discover if water exists on other planets

Part B: Which sentence from the article **best** supports your answer in part A?

(A) "NASA is a group of people that is responsible for space travel and research."

(B) "The pictures showed proof that scientists were right—nothing could live on Mars."

(C) "*Pathfinder* sent more than 16,000 photographs back to Earth."

(D) "They also wanted to know if any plants or animals had ever lived there."

GO ON →

Read the article "Closest Star" before answering Numbers 6 through 10.

Closest Star

A tiny white light twinkles in the night sky and a large yellow ball blazes brightly in the daytime sky. Which of those objects is a star? You answered correctly if you said, "Both!" The daytime light is the sun, of course. It looks very different from the tiny lights you see at night. It is hard to believe that the sun is actually the same kind of object.

A star is a ball of extremely hot gases. The gases are so hot that they burn and glow. As a rule of thumb, a very hot day here on Earth is about 100 degrees. Gases at the sun's surface are about one hundred times hotter than that. Like all stars, the sun is even hotter inside. At the sun's center it is about 27 million degrees!

Stars do not all have the same temperature, however. They differ in color and brightness as well. The hottest stars glow bluish white. The coolest stars glow coppery red. The sun is actually a star of ordinary temperature and brightness. Ordinary stars glow yellow.

Stars are not all the same size either. Some stars are so large that they are called supergiants. Other stars are much smaller. The sun is a star of ordinary size.

Then why does the sun look so much larger than any other star? The sun looks larger because it is so much closer to Earth than any other star. The closer an object is to you, the larger it looks. The sun is about 93 million miles away. That is very far, but it is close if you are talking about distances in the universe. Other stars are much, much farther away. Their light takes a very lengthy time to travel through space and reach Earth.

GO ON →

All in all, our sun is a very ordinary star. However, to us, on Earth, it does not appear that way. To us, the sun is a huge and a bright star.

Just how big is the sun compared to Earth? Think of this visual. If the sun were the size of a basketball, Earth would be the size of the head of a pin! More than a million planets the size of Earth could fit in the sun. There might even be space left over for a moon or two.

The sun's brightness is also powerful to us. It is so bright that you should not look directly at it. If you did, it could damage your eyes. The sun blocks light from the other stars. That is why you cannot see other stars during the day.

Although the sun is an ordinary star in the universe, it is a vitally important star to Earth and its existence.

GO ON →

Now answer Numbers 6 through 10. Base your answers on "Closest Star."

6 This question has two parts. First, answer part A. Then, answer part B.

Part A: What is the main idea of the article?

Ⓐ A star is a ball of extremely hot gases.

Ⓑ The sun is our nearest and most important star.

Ⓒ Not all stars are the same size and temperature.

Ⓓ The sun is an ordinary star compared to other stars.

Part B: Which sentence from the article **best** summarizes the main idea?

Ⓐ "A tiny white light twinkles in the night sky and a large yellow ball blazes brightly in the daytime sky."

Ⓑ "The sun is actually a star of ordinary temperature and brightness."

Ⓒ "More than a million planets the size of Earth could fit in the sun."

Ⓓ "Although the sun is an ordinary star in the universe, it is a vitally important star to Earth and its existence."

7 Read the sentence from the article.

Their light takes a very <u>lengthy</u> time to travel through space and reach Earth.

The suffix -*y* means "full of." What does the word <u>lengthy</u> mean?

Ⓐ average

Ⓑ difficult

Ⓒ long

Ⓓ powerful

GO ON →

8 Underline the sentence that summarizes the main idea of the paragraph.

Then why does the sun look so much larger than any other star? The sun looks larger because it is so much closer to Earth than any other star. The closer an object is to you, the larger it looks. The sun is about 93 million miles away. That is very far, but it is close if you are talking about distances in the universe. Other stars are much, much farther away. Their light takes a very lengthy time to travel through space and reach Earth.

9 This question has two parts. First, answer part A. Then, answer part B.

Part A: Read the sentence from the article.

It is so bright that you should not look directly at it.

The suffix -*ly* means "a certain way." How do you look at the sun if you look directly at it?

(A) You blink at it.

(B) You look right at it.

(C) You squint your eyes at it.

(D) You stare at it for a long time.

Part B: Which word uses the suffix -*ly* in the same way as directly?

(A) bravely

(B) early

(C) jelly

(D) supply

GO ON →

10 With which statements would the author of the article **most likely** agree? Pick **three** choices.

(A) A star is made of hot copper.

(B) Stars do not all look the same.

(C) People would not be alive without the sun.

(D) The sun cannot block light from other stars.

(E) People will never be able to walk on the sun.

(F) The surface of the sun is hotter than its center.

STOP

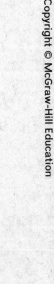

Name: _____ Date: _____

Now answer Number 11. Base your answer on "Mysterious Mars" and "Closest Star."

11 Scientists have done a lot of research on Mars and the sun. What have they discovered? Include information from both articles to support your answer.

_____

_____

_____

_____

_____

_____

_____

_____

_____

_____

_____

_____

_____

Answer Key

Question	Correct Answer	Content Focus	CCSS	Complexity
1A	C	Suffixes: *-y*	L.3.4b	DOK 1
1B	B	Suffixes: *-y*/Text Evidence	L.3.4b/RI.3.1	DOK 1
2	see below	Main Idea and Key Details	RI.3.2	DOK 2
3	B	Suffixes: *-ly*	L.3.4b	DOK 1
4	A, F	Main Idea and Key Details	RI.3.2	DOK 2
5A	C	Main Idea and Key Details	RI.3.2	DOK 2
5B	A	Main Idea and Key Details/Text Evidence	RI.3.2/RI.3.1	DOK 2
6A	B	Main Idea and Key Details	RI.3.2	DOK 2
6B	D	Main Idea and Key Details/Text Evidence	RI.3.2/RI.3.1	DOK 2
7	C	Suffixes: *-y*	L.3.4b	DOK 1
8	see below	Main Idea and Key Details	RI.3.2	DOK 2
9A	B	Suffixes: *-ly*	L.3.4b	DOK 1
9B	A	Suffixes: *-ly*/Text Evidence	L.3.4b/RI.3.1	DOK 1
10	B, C, E	Author's Point of View	RI.3.6	DOK 3
11	see below	Writing About Text	W.3.8	DOK 4

Comprehension 2, 4, 5A, 5B, 6A, 6B, 8, 10	/12	%
Vocabulary 1A, 1B, 3, 7, 9A, 9B	/8	%
Total Weekly Assessment Score	/20	%

2 Students should complete the chart with the following sentences:
- Main Idea: Scientists still have a lot to learn about Mars.
- Details: Mars is similar to Earth in some ways.; NASA has had many missions to Mars.; Plants and animals cannot survive on Mars.

8 Students should underline the following sentence:
- The sun looks larger because it is so much closer to Earth than any other star.

11 To receive full credit for the response, the following information should be included: Scientists have discovered that Mars is a rocky planet. They have looked for water using a powerful telescope and robots, but they have not found any. The freezing temperatures and dust storms make it difficult for life to exist. In fact, they learned that nothing can live on Mars. Scientists have also learned that the sun is a star that is much closer to Earth than other stars. It is made of extremely hot gases. It is also very important to our existence. It provides heat and light to Earth.

Read the article "Beatrix Potter: Lover of Nature" before answering Numbers 1 through 5.

Beatrix Potter: Lover of Nature

Some people love nature. They spend time in it, draw about it, and write about it. Beatrix Potter was like that. Beatrix was born long ago, on July 28, 1866. She lived in a large house in London, England. In those days, well-to-do little girls did not go to school. They were taught at home. Beatrix was no different, and her parents hired a teacher to teach her reading, writing, art, and music.

Beatrix had a little brother named Bertram. Both she and her brother had a schoolroom in the house where they studied. But when Bertram was six, he went away to school. After that, Beatrix was very lonesome since her parents did not allow other children to play with her. So Beatrix was on her own in a very big house. She spent a lot of this time drawing and painting.

During the summers, the Potter family left the noisy city and went to the country. Beatrix loved her time in nature. In the city, the children's freedom was limited. In the country, they could play freely, exploring the forests and meadows. All the time, Beatrix and Bertram drew pictures of everything they saw. They even caught wild animals and tamed them! Some of them they kept as pets. They had rabbits, a snake, a green frog, a tortoise, and two lizards.

Beatrix and Bertram kept a collection of the animals in her schoolroom in London. Beatrix watched them play and eat. She watched them sleep and move. She sketched them constantly. Two of Beatrix's favorite pets were rabbits. She named one Peter Piper and the other Benjamin Bouncer. She often took the rabbits outside on a leash.

GO ON →

When Beatrix was 27, she wrote a letter to a five-year-old child named Noel. Noel was sick, and she wanted to cheer him up. She did not know what to write to the boy. So she remembered her pet rabbits, and an idea came to her out of the blue. She drew pictures of four rabbits and wrote a story about them. It was a great success, and Noel loved it! Later, she made the story into a book called "The Tale of Peter Rabbit." Children enjoyed the story about a naughty rabbit that steals lettuce from a farmer and disobeys his mother. More and more books were printed.

Beatrix wrote other books. Benjamin Bouncer became another rabbit in her stories. She called him Benjamin Bunny. She moved to Hill Top Farm, where she wrote many of her stories. She wrote about the animals on her farm. She made up stories about ducks, hens, dogs, mice, kittens, and cats. She also became a skilled artist. She drew lovely, detailed pictures of plants, mushrooms, and animals. In all, Beatrix Potter wrote 22 excellent books for children.

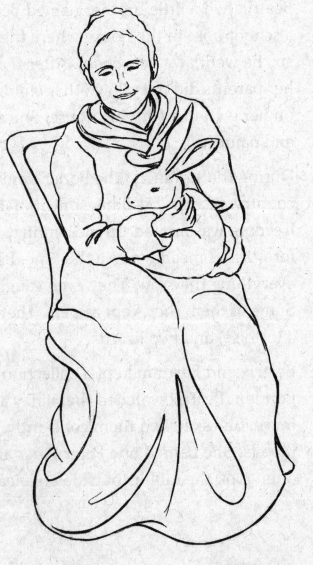

Beatrix loved the countryside and wanted to protect it. So she bought many acres of land with lakes and forests. She died in 1943, but she left her farms and land to the government. Today this land is still protected. You can even visit Hill Top Farm where she once lived.

GO ON →

Now answer Numbers 1 through 5. Base your answers on "Beatrix Potter: Lover of Nature."

1 This question has two parts. First, answer part A. Then, answer part B.

Part A: Which sentence **best** describes the main idea of the article?

Ⓐ Beatrix Potter had many animals that she loved to draw.

Ⓑ Beatrix Potter loved animals and wrote stories about them.

Ⓒ Beatrix Potter liked the country because she could play freely.

Ⓓ Beatrix Potter wrote a story to a sick little boy to cheer him up.

Part B: Which sentence from the article **best** supports your answer in part A?

Ⓐ "She lived in a large house in London, England."

Ⓑ "All the time, Beatrix and Bertram drew pictures of everything they saw."

Ⓒ "Noel was sick, and she wanted to cheer him up."

Ⓓ "She made up stories about ducks, hens, dogs, mice, kittens, and cats."

GO ON →

2 Read the sentences from the article.

But when Bertram was six, he went away to school. After that, Beatrix was very <u>lonesome</u> since her parents did not allow other children to play with her.

Which word shares the **same** root as <u>lonesome</u>?

(A) escape

(B) lonely

(C) longhand

(D) oneself

3 Circle **three** sentences that belong in a summary of the article.

Summary of Article

Beatrix explored forests as a child.

Beatrix wrote many books for children.

Beatrix had a brother named Bertram.

Beatrix became a skilled artist.

Beatrix loved nature and animals.

GO ON →

4 This question has two parts. First, answer part A. Then, answer part B.

Part A: Read the sentence from the article.

Beatrix and Bertram kept a <u>collection</u> of the animals in her schoolroom in London.

What does the word <u>collection</u> tell about the animals?

(A) They were all small.

(B) They were all very pretty.

(C) There was a group of them.

(D) There were very few of them.

Part B: Which word has the same root as <u>collection</u>?

(A) collector

(B) color

(C) contribution

(D) corruption

5 Choose **two** sentences from the article that show the author's point of view.

(A) "In those days, well-to-do little girls did not go to school."

(B) "Both she and her brother had a schoolroom in the house where they studied."

(C) "In the city, the children's freedom was limited."

(D) "They had rabbits, a snake, a green frog, a tortoise, and two lizards."

(E) "Later, she made the story into a book called 'The Tale of Peter Rabbit.'"

(F) "In all, Beatrix Potter wrote 22 excellent books for children."

GO ON →

Read the article "Plants and People" before answering Numbers 6 through 10.

Plants and People

Plants grow almost everywhere there is land on Earth. Even in a city, you will find plants. Trees grow along streets. Grass grows in parks. Weeds grow through cracks in the sidewalk. And that is a good thing because plants give off the oxygen we all breathe. Plants do more than that, however. People have found many uses for this green life that shares our planet.

People use plants for food. Crisp green lettuce, crunchy orange carrots, and yellow sweet corn taste delicious. Juicy apples, blueberries, and oranges make our mouths water. In fact, plants make food for the whole planet. Without plants to eat, people and other animals could not live.

People also wear cloth that is made from plants. Cotton comes from the white puffy seeds of the cotton plant. How many of your clothes are made from cotton? Linen is a soft, light material made from the flax plant. Rayon is another cloth that is made from a plant. A rayon shirt is soft, smooth, and cool.

Another obvious use of plants is for building and making things. Wood comes from trees, and wood is used to build houses and make furniture. Reeds are also useful in making objects. People have woven reeds into baskets and mats for thousands of years. The rubber in your eraser and the cork in a bulletin board come from plants as well.

Many plants are useful for just one thing. Others have almost countless uses. Take bamboo, for example. This strong yet light grass grows very tall very quickly. You can eat it. You can wear it. You can use it to build everything from a bridge to a bike. People have even built cars from bamboo!

GO ON →

Medicine is probably the least known use for plants. Most people have heard of aspirin. Many people take this medicine for pain or when they have a fever. Most people do not know that this medicine comes from plants. Aspirin is made from the bark of the willow tree. Another drug called quinine is made from tree bark. It is used to treat malaria. Malaria is a very serious disease, but it is treatable thanks to plants. People who live in warm climates can get the disease from mosquito bites. Now scientists are testing a new drug to treat this illness. The new medicine comes from a plant, too.

Plants provide so much for people. We should not forget one other important thing plants give us. They give us beauty! Imagine a world without colorful flowers, tall trees, and swaying grasses. Is that a world you would want to live in?

GO ON →

**Now answer Numbers 6 through 10. Base your answers on
"Plants and People."**

6 Complete the chart with the main idea of the article and two
details that support the main idea. Write the correct sentences
from the box. Not all sentences will be used.

Main Idea	Supporting Details

Sentences:

People use plants for food.

People see trees along streets.

People use plants to build things.

People have found many uses for plants.

People often have heard of aspirin as a medicine.

7 Read the sentences from the article.

Reeds are also <u>useful</u> in making objects. People have woven reeds
into baskets and mats for thousands of years.

Which word has the **same** root word as <u>useful</u>?

(A) fully

(B) reuse

(C) selfish

(D) usually

8 Read the paragraph from the article.

Many plants are useful for just one thing. Others have almost countless uses. Take bamboo, for example. This strong yet light grass grows very tall very quickly. You can eat it. You can wear it. You can use it to build everything from a bridge to a bike. People have even built cars from bamboo!

Which statement **best** summarizes the main idea of the paragraph?

(A) Bamboo has many uses for people.

(B) Bamboo has even been used to build cars.

(C) Bamboo is strong yet light enough to carry.

(D) Bamboo grows tall and quickly for farmers to harvest.

9 Read the sentences from the article.

Malaria is a very serious disease, but it is <u>treatable</u> thanks to plants.

Which word has the same root word as <u>treatable</u>?

(A) eaten

(B) timetable

(C) treatment

(D) usable

GO ON →

10 This question has two parts. First, answer part A. Then, answer part B.

Part A: Read the paragraph from the article.

Medicine is probably the least known use for plants. Most people have heard of aspirin. Many people take this medicine for pain or when they have a fever. Most people do not know that this medicine comes from plants. Aspirin is made from the bark of the willow tree. Another drug called quinine is made from tree bark. It is used to treat malaria. Malaria is a very serious disease, but it is treatable thanks to plants. People who live in warm climates can get the disease from mosquito bites. Now scientists are testing a new drug to treat this illness. The new medicine comes from a plant, too.

Which sentence **best** states the main idea of the paragraph?

(A) Plants have many uses for people.

(B) Plants are used to develop medicines.

(C) Medicines are similar to plants in many ways.

(D) There are many plants that we have not discovered yet.

Part B: Pick **two** details that would **best** support the main idea of this paragraph.

(A) Mosquitos come from warm climates.

(B) Some plants have very strange names.

(C) Scientists study plants for new medicines.

(D) People can buy their medicine in local markets.

(E) There is often more than one medicine for an illness.

(F) People chew the bark of the willow tree to get rid of headaches.

Now answer Number 11. Base your answer on "Beatrix Potter: Lover of Nature" and "Plants and People."

11 How do the articles show the positive effect nature has on our lives? Include information from both articles to support your answer.

_____

_____

_____

_____

_____

_____

_____

_____

_____

_____

_____

_____

Answer Key

Name: _____

Question	Correct Answer	Content Focus	CCSS	Complexity
1A	B	Main Idea and Key Details	RI.3.2	DOK 2
1B	D	Main Idea and Key Details/Text Evidence	RI.3.2/ RI.3.1	DOK 2
2	B	Root Words	L.3.4c	DOK 1
3	see below	Main Idea and Key Details	RI.3.2	DOK 2
4A	C	Root Words	L.3.4c	DOK 1
4B	A	Root Words/Text Evidence	L.3.4c/ RI.3.1	DOK 1
5	C, F	Author's Point of View	RI.3.6	DOK 3
6	see below	Main Idea and Key Details	RI.3.2	DOK 2
7	B	Root Words	L.3.4c	DOK 1
8	A	Main Idea and Key Details	RI.3.2	DOK 2
9	C	Root Words	L.3.4c	DOK 1
10A	B	Main Idea and Key Details	RI.3.2	DOK 2
10B	C, F	Main Idea and Key Details/Text Evidence	RI.3.2/ RI.3.1	DOK 2
11	see below	Writing About Text	W.3.8	DOK 4

Comprehension 1A, 1B, 3, 5, 6, 8, 10A, 10B	/12	%
Vocabulary 2, 4A, 4B, 7, 9	/8	%
Total Weekly Assessment Score	/20	%

3 Students should circle the following sentences to include in a summary:
- Beatrix wrote many books for children.
- Beatrix became a skilled artist.
- Beatrix loved nature and animals.

6 Students should complete the chart as follows:
- Main Idea—People have found many uses for plants.
- Supporting Details—People use plants for food.; People use plants to build things.

11 To receive full credit for the response, the following information should be included: Student responses should focus on the following main ideas and provide text evidence: Beatrix Potter's love of nature inspired her to write many books and protect her land. In the article "Plants and People," the author shows that plants provide us with many things that improve our lives.

Read the article "The Silk Road" before answering Numbers 1 through 5.

The Silk Road

Long ago, traders brought treasures from the East to Europe. They were looking for new and amazing goods to sell. Trips to the East became more favorable when traders found silks and spices. These treasures were not the ordinary goods that most traders brought back. People in Western Europe began to prize these finer goods. Soon, more traders began to travel to the East. It was a good way to become wealthy. The route became known as the "Silk Road."

The Silk Road was not really a road. There were no markings that people could follow. It was a system of trade routes from China to the Middle East. There were many routes that traders could follow. Some went over the land, while others went across the sea. No matter which route the traders traveled, there was always danger.

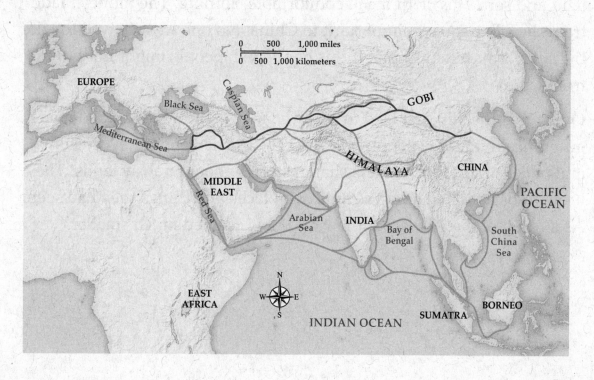

GO ON →

Traders who traveled by land used camels or horses. These animals carried heavy loads, which made the trips manageable. Since there were no marked roads, traders often had a rough journey. First, traders had to cross over the desert. Then they crossed over a high mountain range. Bad weather was also a problem and could slow the traders down. In the desert, they faced hot, dry temperatures and sand storms. Snow and freezing temperatures were a concern in the mountains. Robbers caused trouble, too. These robbers knew that the goods traders carried were worth a fortune. Often, traders were robbed of their goods.

At sea, traders faced terrible storms and high waves. Water and winds often pushed the boats in the wrong direction. Sometimes the ships crashed on land. They also had to deal with pirate attacks. Like land robbers, pirates knew the value of the goods traders carried. They attacked trade ships to steal these goods.

Silk was one of the most popular goods from the East. It came from China. Silk was made from the cocoons of silkworms. Workers pulled fine threads off the cocoons. They wove this material into a cloth that was light and soft. This cloth made comfortable clothing. The money made from the silk trade was important to China. No one was allowed to take the silkworms out of China. If this happened, people might not buy silk from China.

Over time, the Silk Road led to many changes. The goods traded made a difference in the way people lived. People learned about new customs and beliefs. Moreover, traders shared stories about faraway lands. They brought back drawings of the amazing places and things they had seen. As a result of the Silk Road, the world now seemed much smaller.

GO ON →

Name: _____ Date: _____

Now answer Numbers 1 through 5. Base your answers on "The Silk Road."

1 Read the sentence from the article.

Trips to the East became more <u>favorable</u> when traders found silks and spices.

The suffix *-able* means "can be" or "is able." What is a <u>favorable</u> trip?

(A) one that is liked

(B) one that is disliked

(C) one that is changed

(D) one that is canceled

2 How does the author show the rough journey over land?

(A) by comparing the journey over land to the journey over sea

(B) by telling how the Silk Road had no real markings people could follow

(C) by explaining how robbers knew the goods traders carried were valuable

(D) by listing the problems traders faced first in the desert and then in the mountains

GO ON →

3 How does the author show the lasting effect of the Silk Road?

Ⓐ by telling how the Silk Road got its name

Ⓑ by listing the changes that happened over time

Ⓒ by explaining the importance of silk traveling by sea

Ⓓ by contrasting the goods from the East with those from the West

4 Read the sentences from the article.

They wove this material into a cloth that was light and soft. This cloth made <u>comfortable</u> clothing.

Which words in the box use the suffix -*able* in the same way as <u>comfortable</u>? Write all the words with the suffix -*able* in the chart.

Words with Suffix -*able*

allowable	cable	likeable	manageable	vegetable

GO ON →

Name: _____ Date: _____

5 This question has two parts. First, answer part A. Then, answer part B.

Part A: How does the author help the reader understand how silk was made?

(A) by comparing silk to other materials

(B) by explaining how it affected the silkworms

(C) by listing the steps it took to make the material

(D) by comparing the types of clothes it could be used for

Part B: Which sentences from the article **best** support your answer in part A? Pick **two** sentences.

(A) "Silk was one of the most popular goods from the East."

(B) "Silk was made from the cocoons of silkworms."

(C) "Workers pulled fine threads off the cocoons."

(D) "They wove this material into a cloth that was light and soft."

(E) "The money made from the silk trade was important to China."

(F) "No one was allowed to take the silkworms out of China."

GO ON →

Read the article "Squanto" before answering Numbers 6 through 10.

Squanto

In December of 1620, the Pilgrims landed in North America. Plymouth, as they named it, was a cold and difficult place. The Pilgrims were unprepared to deal with this "New World." Almost half of their group did not survive that winter. Those who lived thought about going back to England. However, they met a Native American who helped them learn to survive in their harsh new home. His name was Tisquantum, or "Squanto."

Squanto lived with a nearby tribe. He soon became friends with the Pilgrims. Squanto showed them how to farm and catch fish. He helped make a peace treaty that was acceptable to both the Pilgrims and the nearby Native Americans.

But how was Squanto able to teach the Pilgrims how to survive? How were his words understandable to them? Squanto spoke English. He learned English several years before while he was in England and Spain. He had not gone to those places by his own choice. He had been taken there against his will.

Years earlier, in 1605, an English sea captain was exploring the North American coast. He captured several Native Americans. Among the captives was Squanto. He was only a young man then. Squanto was taken to England. There he came to live with a rich man named Gorges.

Gorges taught Squanto English. He hired Squanto as a guide. Squanto returned to North America in 1614 to help one of Gorges's men map the coast. He persuaded a group of Native Americans to trade with some of the Englishmen. Because he spoke the languages of both sides, he played a major role in the trading.

GO ON →

Once again, however, Squanto was torn from his homeland. He and twenty-six other Native Americans were captured by a man named Thomas Hunt. Hunt set sail for Spain. There he tried to sell the captured men into slavery. Squanto and the others were saved from this fate by a group of priests.

Squanto lived in Spain with these priests for a few years. Then, in 1618, he tried to return to his people. Someone in North America recognized him from his time in England. The man believed Squanto still belonged to Gorges, so he was sent back to England. Gorges welcomed him as a dependable friend, whom he had known and trusted for a long time. He arranged for Squanto to join a trading group going to North America. They agreed that Squanto would stay in his home in North America as a free man.

In 1619, Squanto finally arrived at his village. No one was there. A disease had killed his people. Saddened, Squanto went to live with a neighboring Native American group. Then he heard that English colonists settled where his old village had once been.

On March 22, 1621, Squanto went to meet the Pilgrims. He became their teacher and saved them from starving. He became their interpreter. Squanto worked hard for peaceable relations between Native Americans and these newcomers. As a result, he helped save them from war. If not for Squanto, the story of the Pilgrims in the New World would be much different.

GO ON →

Name: _____ Date: _____

Now answer Numbers 6 through 10. Base your answers on "Squanto."

6 Read the sentence from the article.

He helped make a peace treaty that was <u>acceptable</u> to both the Pilgrims and the nearby Native Americans.

If *accept* means "agree," what does <u>acceptable</u> mean?

(A) can agree to

(B) cannot agree to

(C) not wanting to agree

(D) make someone agree

7 Arrange the events from the passage in the correct sequence. Write the sentences in the correct order in the chart below.

1	
2	
3	
4	

Events:
Gorges frees Squanto in 1618.
Squanto lives with priests in Spain.
Squanto goes back to his village and finds it empty.
Squanto helps one of Gorges's men map the coast of North America.

GO ON →

8 Read the sentence from the article.

Gorges welcomed him as a <u>dependable</u> friend, whom he had known and trusted for a long time.

What does the word <u>dependable</u> mean?

(A) can be trusted

(B) trusting of others

(C) cannot be trusted

(D) cannot trust others

9 Which text evidence shows that the Pilgrims' lives were different after meeting Squanto? Pick **two** choices.

(A) "Almost half of their group did not survive that winter."

(B) "Squanto lived with a nearby tribe."

(C) "Squanto showed them how to farm and catch fish."

(D) "Among the captives was Squanto."

(E) "On March 22, 1621, Squanto went to meet the Pilgrims."

(F) "He became their teacher and saved them from starving."

GO ON →

Name: _____ Date: _____

10 This question has two parts. First, answer part A. Then, answer part B.

Part A: Read the paragraph from the article.

On March 22, 1621, Squanto went to meet the Pilgrims. He became their teacher and saved them from starving. He became their interpreter. Squanto worked hard for peaceable relations between Native Americans and these newcomers. As a result, he helped save them from war. If not for Squanto, the story of the Pilgrims in the New World would be much different.

What is the **most** important idea of this paragraph?

Ⓐ Squanto met the Pilgrims in 1621.

Ⓑ Squanto helped the Pilgrims.

Ⓒ Squanto was a hard worker.

Ⓓ Squanto worked for peace.

Part B: Which sentence from the paragraph **best** states the main idea?

Ⓐ "He became their interpreter."

Ⓑ "Squanto worked hard for peaceable relations between Native Americans and these newcomers."

Ⓒ "As a result, he helped save them from war."

Ⓓ "If not for Squanto, the story of the Pilgrims in the New World would be much different."

178   Grade 3   **Weekly Assessment** · Unit 3, Week 5

Name: _____ Date: _____

Now answer Number 11. Base your answer on "The Silk Road" and "Squanto."

11 How did the traders in "The Silk Road" and Squanto both affect events in history? Include information from both articles to support your answer.

_____

_____

_____

_____

_____

_____

_____

_____

_____

_____

_____

_____

Answer Key

Name: _____

Question	Correct Answer	Content Focus	CCSS	Complexity
1	A	Suffixes: *-able*	L.3.4b	DOK 1
2	D	Text Structure: Sequence	RI.3.8	DOK 2
3	B	Text Structure: Sequence	RI.3.8	DOK 2
4	see below	Suffixes: *-able*	L.3.4b	DOK 1
5A	C	Text Structure: Sequence	RI.3.8	DOK 2
5B	C, D	Text Structure: Sequence/Text Evidence	RI.3.8/ RI.3.1	DOK 2
6	A	Suffixes: *-able*	L.3.4b	DOK 1
7	see below	Text Structure: Sequence	RI.3.3	DOK 1
8	A	Suffixes: *-able*	L.3.4b	DOK 1
9	C, F	Text Structure: Sequence	RI.3.8	DOK 2
10A	B	Main Idea and Key Details	RI.3.2	DOK 2
10B	D	Main Idea and Key Details/Text Evidence	RI.3.2/ RI.3.1	DOK 2
11	see below	Writing About Text	W.3.8	DOK 4

Comprehension 2, 3, 5A, 5B, 7, 9, 10A, 10B	/12	%
Vocabulary 1, 4, 6, 8	/8	%
Total Weekly Assessment Score	/20	%

4 Students should complete the chart with the following words:
- allowable
- likeable
- manageable

7 Students should put the events in the following order:
- 1— Squanto helps one of Gorges's men map the coast of North America.
- 2— Squanto lives with priests in Spain.
- 3— Gorges frees Squanto in 1618.
- 4— Squanto goes back to his village and finds it empty.

11 To receive full credit for the response, the following information should be included: The traders brought new customs, ideas, and stories from the East that changed the way people all over the world lived. Squanto helped the Pilgrims settle in the New World and helped save them from war. The Pilgrims might not have survived without Squanto's help.

Read the passage "Food for Thought" before answering Numbers 1 through 5.

Food for Thought

Ronelle and Deon tagged along after their father at the grocery store. Ronelle was in charge of watching her excitable little brother. Her father did not want him knocking things over or wandering off in the busy store. With cans stacked almost ceiling high and walls of boxes blocking her view, it was not an easy task.

"Dad, hey Dad," Deon said as he tugged on his father's sweater. "Can we buy something good to eat too?"

"Sure," his father mumbled, as he carefully inspected the label on a box of cereal. "Just be sure it's healthy for you."

"Yay!" Deon cheered. Almost immediately he pulled a box of Cheesy Potato Doodles from the middle of a stack. Ronelle dove to keep the top boxes from tumbling over. Then she looked at Deon.

"Don't you remember the time you ate almost a whole bag of those at Sam's birthday party? They made you sick!" she reminded him.

"Oh, right," Deon spoke thoughtfully. He handed the box to Ronelle, who replaced it lightly on top of the others.

In the next lane, Deon spotted bags of Crunchy Cracker Sticks piled in a pyramid. This time, just lifting the top bag caused the others to begin sliding downward on the slippery slope. Ronelle jumped into action and stopped the slide.

Now it was her turn to recall an unpleasant memory. "I ate those once," she told Deon. "They're so salty, and they made me really thirsty. I had to drink a million glasses of water afterward!"

GO ON →

"Oh," Deon said. He handed the bag to Ronelle, who didn't even try to put it atop the others. Instead, she leaned it on the side of the pile.

Then, Deon's eyes widened when he saw the frozen food section, and he darted over to it, almost knocking into a woman and her cart.

"Juicy Poparoos! Juicy Poparoos! I saw them on TV! I want them!" Deon shouted.

Ronelle took a carton out of the freezer and read the label to Deon. "The very first ingredient is sugar. In fact, Juicy Poparoos are nothing but sugar, water, and food coloring," said Ronelle.

"Do you remember the last time you went to the dentist? You had to have a cavity filled. Do you want to go through that again?"

"No," Deon said.

Then Ronelle noticed the fruit section nearby. Bunches of plump red grapes caught her eye.

"How about some grapes instead? They're naturally sweet, and juicy, too!" Ronelle suggested.

"Great!" said Deon.

"Phew!" thought Ronelle.

GO ON →

Now answer Numbers 1 through 5. Base your answers on "Food for Thought."

1 This question has two parts. First, answer part A. Then, answer part B.

Part A: Read the sentence from the passage.

He handed the box to Ronelle, who <u>replaced</u> it lightly on top of the others.

What does the word <u>replaced</u> **most likely** mean?

(A) put back

(B) held back

(C) threw back

(D) looked back

Part B: Which word has the **same** root as <u>replaced</u>?

(A) acted

(B) placement

(C) replay

(D) shoelace

GO ON →

2 Write **one** sentence from the passage that supports the information in the chart. Choose from the list below the chart.

Narrator	an outside narrator
Text Evidence	

Text Evidence:

"Ronelle and Deon tagged along after their father at the grocery store."

"'Can we buy something good to eat too?'"

"'Do you remember the last time you went to the dentist?'"

3 Read the sentence from the passage.

Then, Deon's eyes <u>widened</u> when he saw the frozen food section, and he darted over to it, almost knocking into a woman and her cart.

Which word has the **same** root word as <u>widened</u>?

(A) dented

(B) ended

(C) wider

(D) wisely

GO ON →

4 This question has two parts. First, answer part A. Then, answer part B.

Part A: Which word **best** describes Ronelle?

Ⓐ bored

Ⓑ bossy

Ⓒ responsible

Ⓓ rude

Part B: Which sentence from the passage **best** supports your answer in part A?

Ⓐ "Her father did not want him knocking things over or wandering off in the busy store."

Ⓑ "'Don't you remember the time you ate almost a whole bag of those at Sam's birthday party?'"

Ⓒ "In the next lane, Deon spotted bags of Crunchy Cracker Sticks piled in a pyramid."

Ⓓ "'In fact, Juicy Poparoos are nothing but sugar, water, and food coloring,' said Ronelle."

5 With which statements would Ronelle **most likely** agree? Pick **two** choices.

Ⓐ Snacks high in sugar are bad for you.

Ⓑ Getting a cavity filled is not that bad.

Ⓒ Juicy Poparoos can be a healthy snack.

Ⓓ Fruits are good for you and taste good, too.

Ⓔ Any snack is fine if you don't eat a lot of it.

Ⓕ It is easy to be in charge of a younger brother.

GO ON →

Read the passage "Take Time" before answering Numbers 6 through 10.

Take Time

It was Tuesday morning and Jake's mother was driving him to school. As usual, they were cruising down busy Fortieth Street. Jake's mother was driving as fast as the speed limit and traffic allowed. Jake sat in the back seat, daydreaming as he looked out the window. They were passing a city park, and it flew past him in a blur.

"That park is blocking our way," Jake's mother complained. "If I could drive right through it, we'd be at school in no time, but I have to drive all the way around it."

The next day, as customary, Jake's mother was driving him to school. Jake was looking out the window, but his thoughts were elsewhere. Suddenly, he saw something shoot up from out of the trees. Just as quickly, it disappeared. At least, he *thought* he saw something, but they had sped by so quickly that he was uncertain.

The following day, once again Jake and his mother were on their way to school. This time, Jake tried to focus his eyes carefully as they passed the park. Tree after blurry tree rushed by, when—there! There it was again!

"Mom, I just saw something shoot up out of the park!" he exclaimed. "I think it was a huge jet of water."

"Really, honey?" his mother murmured. She was thinking of the things she needed to do at work once Jake was dropped off safely at school.

"Can we go back and see?" he asked.

"No, we don't have time. You've got a busy day at school, and I have too much to do today myself."

Copyright © McGraw-Hill Education

GO ON →

The following day, Jake waited and watched until he knew they were close to the spot. Luckily, traffic had begun to slow for a stoplight up ahead. Just as the water whooshed up, Jake hollered, "Look, Mom! Look!"

His mother caught a glimpse out of the corner of her eye. "That is strange!" she said.

"Can we please go see what it is?" Jake begged.

"Not today, but tomorrow is Saturday. We'll stop by the park on our way to your soccer practice to uncover this mystery," she promised.

On Saturday morning, Jake and his mother strolled into the park and down a wooded path. Approaching the middle of the park, they discovered a large and lovely water fountain. Every so often, it would spurt a burst of water high into the air. "Mom, this is what I saw shooting up out of the park on our way to school!" Jake exclaimed.

Jake's mother's face was beaming. "What an enjoyable walk! It feels so good to stretch my legs. Let's come here more often," she suggested. "In fact, we don't always have to drive to school. Let's walk to school when the weather is nice, and we can walk through this park on our way."

"Sure!" Jake happily agreed.

GO ON →

Now answer Numbers 6 through 10. Base your answers on "Take Time."

6 This question has two parts. First, answer part A. Then, answer part B.

Part A: How does Jake's mother feel at the beginning of the passage?

Ⓐ angry

Ⓑ happy

Ⓒ relaxed

Ⓓ rushed

Part B: Which sentence **best** supports your answer in part A?

Ⓐ "It was Tuesday morning and Jake's mother was driving him to school."

Ⓑ "As usual, they were cruising down busy Fortieth Street."

Ⓒ "Jake's mother was driving as fast as the speed limit and traffic allowed."

Ⓓ "Jake sat in the back seat, daydreaming as he looked out the window."

7 Read the sentence from the passage.

The next day, as customary, Jake's mother was driving him to school.

Which word has the **same** root word as customary?

Ⓐ accustomed

Ⓑ costume

Ⓒ custard

Ⓓ marry

GO ON →

8 Pick **three** words that show how Jake feels when his mother does not stop the car while driving past the park.

Ⓐ angry

Ⓑ confused

Ⓒ disappointed

Ⓓ frightened

Ⓔ frustrated

Ⓕ nervous

9 This question has two parts. First, answer part A. Then, answer part B.

Part A: Read the sentences from the passage.

This time, Jake tried to focus his eyes carefully as they passed the park. Tree after blurry tree rushed by, when—there! There it was again!

The root word in blurry can mean "dim" or "hard to see." What would a blurry tree look like?

Ⓐ not bloomed

Ⓑ very green

Ⓒ not clear

Ⓓ very tall

Part B: Which other word has the **same** root word as blurry?

Ⓐ blunt

Ⓑ blurred

Ⓒ burro

Ⓓ bury

GO ON →

10 The story is told by an outside narrator, and not Jake or his mother. Underline **two** sentences in the paragraph that clearly show that Jake and his mother are not narrating the story.

On Saturday morning, Jake and his mother strolled into the park and down a wooded path. Approaching the middle of the park, they discovered a large and lovely water fountain. Every so often, it would spurt a burst of water high into the air. "Mom, this is what I saw shooting up out of the park on our way to school!" Jake exclaimed.

Name: _____ Date: _____

Now answer Number 11. Base your answer on "Food for Thought" and "Take Time."

11 How do the points of view of Deon and Jake's mother change in the passages? Include details from both passages to support your answer.

_____

_____

_____

_____

_____

_____

_____

_____

_____

_____

_____

_____

Answer Key

Name: _____

Question	Correct Answer	Content Focus	CCSS	Complexity
1A	A	Root Words	L.3.4c	DOK 1
1B	B	Root Words/Text Evidence	L.3.4c/ RL.3.1	DOK 1
2	see below	Point of View	RL.3.6	DOK 2
3	C	Root Words	L.3.4c	DOK 1
4A	C	Character, Setting, Plot: Character	RL.3.3	DOK 2
4B	D	Character, Setting, Plot: Character/ Text Evidence	RL.3.3/ RL.3.1	DOK 2
5	A, D	Point of View	RL.3.6	DOK 3
6A	D	Point of View	RL.3.6	DOK 3
6B	C	Point of View/Text Evidence	RL.3.6/ RL.3.1	DOK 3
7	A	Root Words	L.3.4c	DOK 1
8	B, C, E	Point of View	RL.3.6	DOK 3
9A	C	Root Words	L.3.4c	DOK 1
9B	B	Root Words/Text Evidence	L.3.4c/ RL.3.1	DOK 1
10	see below	Point of View	RL.3.6	DOK 2
11	see below	Writing About Text	W.3.8	DOK 4

Comprehension 2, 4A, 4B, 5, 6A, 6B, 8, 10	/12	%
Vocabulary 1A, 1B, 3, 7, 9A, 9B	/8	%
Total Weekly Assessment Score	/20	%

2 Students should complete the chart with the following text evidence:
- "Ronelle and Deon tagged along after their father at the grocery store."

10 Students should underline the following sentences:
- On Saturday morning, Jake and his mother strolled into the park and down a wooded path.
- Approaching the middle of the park, they discovered a large and lovely water fountain.

11 To receive full credit for the response, the following information should be included: Deon learns that snack foods are not healthy because they can make you sick, thirsty, and cause cavities. He also learns that some healthy foods can be naturally sweet. Jake's mother learns to slow down and enjoy the moment. She discovers that walking through the park is a good idea because it gives her a chance to exercise and relax.

Read the passage "Playground Games" before answering Numbers 1 through 5.

Playground Games

On the hottest day of school, I didn't want to go out on the playground and play soccer. There was no shade, no wind—only the boiling sun. And even worse, there were two of my classmates who just can't get along. They spend every recess arguing. They are very disrespectful to each other. As soon as I got out to the playground, I saw them staring each other down. I decided I was tired of them arguing and was going to do something about it.

Angel, the tallest girl in our grade was face to face with Leonard. They were yelling in each other's faces when I walked right up and got between them.

"Enough!" I cried.

But Angel just ignored me. I thought about that for a second and then I did something unexpected. I spun around like a dancer and froze in an odd position without moving a muscle, a goofy look frozen on my face.

"Tanisha, what are you doing?" Angel snarled. "Stop this nonsense, you are acting so strange!"

Leonard suddenly started laughing. "Look at her! She's a statue." He walked over and touched me, and I suddenly unfroze and started dancing again.

"Let's play Freeze Tag," I suggested. "I'm it, and if I touch you, you have to freeze in whatever position you are in."

For a second, he looked at me like I was crazy. Then he took off and I ran after him. Leonard dodged left and right, but I knew it was impossible for him to outrun me. I froze him like he was a flying squirrel, and then left him frozen to try and freeze my other friends.

GO ON →

Suddenly everyone was playing. Kids who usually couldn't get along were having so much fun together. The teachers couldn't believe their eyes. Everyone was playing and no one was arguing.

I told everyone that Freeze Tag was just a preview of other games. After Freeze Tag was over, I showed them how to play Red Rover. Soon a team of kids sang out, "Red Rover, Red Rover, let Angel come over!" We even played Spud, where you call out a person's name and then toss a ball into the air really high. Everybody runs and the person who was called out had to catch it and then touch one of the others with the ball. After that, there was Red Light, Green Light where we all moved around quickly. When someone shouted, "Red Light!" you had to stop instantly. Half the time you just fell on your face laughing. Thanks to everyone playing together, my playground was once again fun!

When the teachers blew the whistle at the end of recess we all headed inside. The class lined up at the drinking fountain. I noticed Angel and Leonard laughing as they were waiting in line. I was happy to see them finally getting along.

GO ON →

Now answer Numbers 1 through 5. Base your answers on "Playground Games."

1 This question has two parts. First, answer part A. Then, answer part B.

Part A: Read the paragraph from the passage.

"Tanisha, what are you doing?" Angel snarled. "Stop this <u>nonsense</u>, you are acting so strange!"

What does the word <u>nonsense</u> **most likely** mean?

Ⓐ Tanisha is not making sense.

Ⓑ Tanisha is making a lot of sense.

Ⓒ Tanisha was making sense earlier.

Ⓓ Tanisha keeps making sense over and over.

Part B: Which word has the same prefix as <u>nonsense</u>?

Ⓐ none

Ⓑ nonstop

Ⓒ sensible

Ⓓ recent

2 What would the reader **most likely** know if the passage were written from Angel's point of view? Pick **two** choices.

Ⓐ which game Leonard likes best

Ⓑ why Leonard laughs at Tanisha

Ⓒ why Leonard is fighting with her

Ⓓ who taught Tanisha how to play soccer

Ⓔ who Tanisha will play with after school

Ⓕ which of Tanisha's games she likes best

GO ON →

3 Draw a line to match Tanisha's point of view on the left with the text evidence that supports it on the right.

Point of View

| Wants to try something new |

| Has a lot of fun while playing |

| Is tired of hearing Angel and Leonard argue |

| Feels good about recess |

Text Evidence

| "I was happy to see them finally getting along." |

| "Half the time you just fell on your face laughing." |

| "'Enough!' I cried." |

| "I told everyone that Freeze Tag was just a preview of other games." |

4 Read the sentence from the passage.

He walked over and touched me, and I suddenly <u>unfroze</u> and started dancing again.

What does the word <u>unfroze</u> mean in this sentence?

Ⓐ to become stiff

Ⓑ to become cold

Ⓒ to become able to move

Ⓓ to become stuck in place

GO ON →

5 This question has two parts. First, answer part A. Then, answer part B.

Part A: What does Tanisha think about recess at the end of the passage?

Ⓐ It is a lot of fun.

Ⓑ It needs to change.

Ⓒ It should be shorter.

Ⓓ It needs more games to play.

Part B: Which sentence from the passage **best** supports your answer in part A?

Ⓐ "Thanks to everyone playing together, my playground was once again fun!"

Ⓑ "When the teachers blew the whistle at the end of recess we all headed inside."

Ⓒ "The class lined up at the drinking fountain."

Ⓓ "I noticed Angel and Leonard laughing as they were waiting in line."

GO ON →

Read the passage "The Bounce in the Ball" before answering Numbers 6 through 10.

The Bounce in the Ball

I couldn't even look at my basketball shoes, much less my ball. They are sitting in my closet, waiting. On Sunday morning, my team is playing a game and I'm supposed to be ready to play basketball. I love the game so much that I asked for a basketball for my birthday when I was still in preschool. I have posters of all the pro and college stars on the walls of my room, but lately I've started to rethink if I want to be on the team.

My father used to be the captain of his school team. Almost every night, I go out to the backyard and shoot baskets with my dad. Lately, I've missed every shot. I can't dribble, and my dad just doesn't understand.

"C'mon, it's easy!" my father loves to say. "Just feel the bounce in the ball."

I can't stand anyone watching me practice, so I asked my older sister to drive me to the park. I wanted to do my own preparation where no one could see me play. My sister is not much of a basketball fan and likes to read a book while I'm on the court, so I know she will leave me alone.

When we got to the playground, we saw that it was empty except for a boy in a wheelchair and his mom. The boy was about my age. I started shooting, but couldn't even hit the rim.

"You need to put your legs into your shot!" the boy shouted to me. I didn't want to be unkind but I thought, "Who is this guy? I've been playing basketball since I could pick up a ball. Does he think I'm a beginner?"

He rolled his chair over to me. "I know what you're thinking. Why is a guy in a wheelchair telling me what I should do with my legs?" He motioned for the ball, and then he made a move so fast that I couldn't believe it. From thirty feet away, he tossed the ball in the basket. He made his wheelchair spin as he did it.

GO ON →

"I'm Pablo. Because I can't jump, I've got to shoot it twice as hard. You can use your legs, so let them push the ball up so you jump first, then shoot." He made shot after shot, over and over, nonstop.

I didn't know what to say, so I took the ball and jumped as high as I could. At the very top, I let the ball go. It hit the backboard and rolled off the edge of the rim.

"Now, that's an improvement!" Pablo told me. I didn't say anything because I was embarrassed. He started to roll away. "I can tell you want to practice alone, so I'll see you later."

"No, wait!" I begged him. "My dad says I have to feel the bounce in the ball." He smiled and caught the pass I threw him. "If you feel the bounce, you're a real player. C'mon, let's show your *papi* you got game."

Pablo and I played every day that week. He showed me how to pretend to go one way and then race past anyone trying to stop me. I learned to put my back to the basket so no one could block my shot. A few days later, on Saturday night, shooting with my dad, I hit ten straight shots. His jaw dropped open. He just stood there, immovable.

"Where'd you learn that?" he asked.

"It's all in the bounce of the ball, Dad."

Copyright © McGraw-Hill Education

Now answer Numbers 6 through 10. Base your answers on "The Bounce in the Ball."

6 This question has two parts. First, answer part A. Then, answer part B.

Part A: Read the sentence from the passage.

I love the game so much that I asked for a basketball for my birthday when I was still in <u>preschool</u>.

What does the word <u>preschool</u> suggest about the narrator?

(A) He asked for a basketball in the evening.

(B) He asked for a basketball in the morning.

(C) He asked for a basketball when he was older.

(D) He asked for a basketball when he was very young.

Part B: Which word has the same prefix as found in <u>preschool</u>?

(A) preheat

(B) president

(C) pressing

(D) schoolhouse

7 How does the narrator feel about his problem at the beginning of the passage? Pick **two** choices.

(A) comfortable

(B) curious

(C) determined

(D) embarrassed

(E) lucky

(F) tired

GO ON →

Name: _____ Date: _____

8 What is the narrator's point of view about basketball at different parts of the story? Choose the correct sentences and write them in the chart. Not all sentences will be used.

Part of Story	Point of View
Beginning	
Middle	
End	

Sentences:

It helps to practice basketball with someone.

It helps to play sports other than basketball.

Basketball is not that hard.

Basketball is very hard.

GO ON →

9 Read the sentences from the passage.

His jaw dropped open. He just stood there, <u>immovable</u>.

What does the word <u>immovable</u> **most likely** mean?

(A) playing fair

(B) standing still

(C) talking loudly

(D) moving around

10 This question has two parts. First, answer part A. Then, answer part B.

Part A: Which sentence **best** describes the lesson of the passage?

(A) Basketball is a very difficult sport.

(B) You should try to beat your father at sports.

(C) Accepting help is a good way to reach your goal.

(D) Treat others the way you would like others to treat you.

Part B: Which sentence from the passage **best** supports your answer in part A?

(A) "He motioned for the ball, and then he made a move so fast that I couldn't believe it."

(B) "He smiled and caught the pass I threw him."

(C) "Pablo and I played every day that week."

(D) "He showed me how to pretend to go one way and then race past anyone trying to stop me."

Name: _____ Date: _____

Now answer Number 11. Base your answer on "Playground Games" and "The Bounce in the Ball."

11 In both passages, Tanisha and Pablo change someone's point of view. Explain how they are able to do this. Include details from both passages to support your answer.

_____

_____

_____

_____

_____

_____

_____

_____

_____

_____

_____

_____

_____

_____

_____

Answer Key

Name: _____

Question	Correct Answer	Content Focus	CCSS	Complexity
1A	A	Prefixes: *non-*	L.3.4b	DOK 1
1B	B	Prefixes: *non-*/Text Evidence	L.3.4b/ RL.3.1	DOK 1
2	C, F	Point of View	RL.3.6	DOK 3
3	see below	Point of View	RL.3.6	DOK 3
4	C	Prefixes: *un-*	L.3.4b	DOK 1
5A	A	Point of View	RL.3.6	DOK 3
5B	A	Point of View/Text Evidence	RL.3.6/ RL.3.1	DOK 3
6A	D	Prefixes: *pre-*	L.3.4b	DOK 1
6B	A	Prefixes: *pre-*/Text Evidence	L.3.4b/ RL.3.1	DOK 1
7	C, D	Point of View	RL.3.6	DOK 3
8	see below	Point of View	RL.3.6	DOK 3
9	B	Prefixes: *im-*	L.3.4b	DOK 1
10A	C	Theme	RL.3.2	DOK 3
10B	D	Theme/Text Evidence	RL.3.2/ RL.3.1	DOK 3
11	see below	Writing About Text	W.3.8	DOK 4

Comprehension 2, 3, 5A, 5B, 7, 8, 10A, 10B	/12	%
Vocabulary 1A, 1B, 4, 6A, 6B, 9	/8	%
Total Weekly Assessment Score	/20	%

3 Students should make the following matches between point of view and text evidence:
- Wants to try something new—"I told everyone that Freeze Tag was just a preview of other games."
- Has a lot of fun while playing—"Half the time you just fell on your face laughing."
- Is tired of hearing Angel and Leonard argue—"'Enough!' I cried."
- Feels good about recess—"I was happy to see them finally getting along."

8 Students should complete the chart with the following sentences:
- Beginning—Basketball is very hard.
- Middle—It helps to practice basketball with someone.
- End—Basketball is not that hard.

11 To receive full credit for the response, the following information should be included: Tanisha helps her friends realize that by playing together and having fun, friends forget about their differences. Pablo helps the narrator in "The Bounce in the Ball" realize it is alright to ask for help and that we all need help with something sometimes.

Read the article "Life in the Cold" before answering Numbers 1 through 5.

Life in the Cold

Picture a place that is covered by ice. A fierce, strong wind blows often, and the weather is always freezing. This is Antarctica, the coldest place on Earth. It might not look like a desert, but it is a dry place. Antarctica gets less than two inches of snowfall each year.

Antarctica is a harsh, or rough, land where it is difficult to live. Scientists are the only people who call it home. Plants cannot grow in the ice. Penguins, seals, and whales are some of the animals that live in Antarctica. How can they live in this frozen, ice-cold land? These animals have special ways to stay warm and find food.

The penguin is a kind of bird. Like all birds, the penguin has several layers of feathers. The feathers closest to the body are called down. These feathers are soft, which helps keep the warmer air next to the penguin's skin.

GO ON →

Penguins also have fat under their skin, called blubber, that protects them from the cold air. Penguins stay warm in another way, too. When it is very cold, hundreds of penguins stand together in a group. They huddle close beside each other with their bodies touching. They share the heat from their bodies to stay warm.

Even though the penguin is a bird, it cannot fly. It has flippers instead of wings. It also has short legs and webbed feet. The flippers and webbed feet help penguins swim. They speed through the water hunting for fish to eat. These birds are graceful swimmers, but penguins have an odd walk on land. They shuffle, or drag their feet, on the ice as they move from place to place.

Seals also live in Antarctica. They are very much like penguins. Seals also have blubber under their skin. They live on land and swim in the sea. They eat fish like penguins, too. However, seals are different from penguins in several ways. A seal's body is covered in thick fur that helps keep the seal warm. Also, a seal has two sets of flippers. One set is on its chest, and the other is on its tail.

Some whales swim in the cold Antarctic waters. Like the other Antarctic animals, whales have lots of blubber to help keep them warm. Even though these huge animals live in water, they are mammals and need to breathe air. Whales dive under the water to feed on shrimp, crabs, and other small sea animals. Whales must be careful when they come up to get air. If they get trapped under a sheet of ice, they cannot breathe.

It is hard to picture a place where it is always winter. Ice stretches out for miles and miles. It is an uncomfortable place for most people to live, yet the Antarctic animals seem right at home.

GO ON →

Now answer Numbers 1 through 5. Base your answers on "Life in the Cold."

1 This question has two parts. First, answer part A. Then, answer part B.

Part A: Read the paragraph from the article.

Even though the penguin is a bird, it cannot fly. It has flippers instead of wings. It also has short legs and webbed feet. The flippers and webbed feet help penguins swim. They speed through the water hunting for fish to eat. These birds are graceful swimmers, but penguins have an odd walk on land. They shuffle, or drag their feet, on the ice as they move from place to place.

What does the author contrast in the paragraph?

- (A) how penguins move in water and on land
- (B) the different ways penguins move on the ice
- (C) how penguins get food in the water and on land
- (D) the way penguins use their flippers and their wings

Part B: Which sentence from the paragraph **best** states this contrast?

- (A) "Even though the penguin is a bird, it cannot fly."
- (B) "It also has short legs and webbed feet."
- (C) "They speed through the water hunting for fish to eat."
- (D) "These birds are graceful swimmers, but penguins have an odd walk on land."

GO ON →

2 Read the sentence from the article.

They <u>huddle</u> close beside each other with their bodies touching.

What does the word <u>huddle</u> **most likely** mean?

- Ⓐ flap wings up and down
- Ⓑ jump into the water
- Ⓒ get in a straight line
- Ⓓ crowd together

3 This question has two parts. First, answer part A. Then, answer part B.

Part A: Read the sentence from the article.

They <u>shuffle</u>, or drag their feet, on the ice as they move from place to place.

What does the word <u>shuffle</u> mean in the sentence?

- Ⓐ to run very fast
- Ⓑ to hop on one foot
- Ⓒ to take large steps
- Ⓓ to walk without lifting the feet

Part B: Which word from the sentence is the **best** clue to the meaning of <u>shuffle</u>?

- Ⓐ drag
- Ⓑ ice
- Ⓒ move
- Ⓓ place

GO ON →

4 How does the author help the reader learn about penguins? Pick **two** choices.

Ⓐ by comparing penguins to people

Ⓑ by comparing penguins to other birds

Ⓒ by describing what penguins look like

Ⓓ by explaining how penguins breathe underwater

Ⓔ by describing different types of penguins in the wild

Ⓕ by explaining the different types of food penguins hunt

5 Compare and contrast penguins and seals. Complete the chart by sorting details about the animals found in the list. Write all of the details from the list in the chart.

Penguins	
Seals	
Both	

Details:

Have blubber	Cannot walk well
Have thick fur	Live in Antarctica
Have short legs	Have two sets of flippers

GO ON →

Read the article "Life Underwater" before answering Numbers 6 through 10.

Life Underwater

Do you know what life is like under the waves? A coral reef is one of the best places to go. The water is warm, and there are lots of fish to see. However, few humans ever visit another part of the ocean—the deep sea. It is a cold, strange world. It is very different from a coral reef.

Creatures of the Sea

Coral reefs are called the rain forests of the ocean. The largest reef in the world is the massive Great Barrier Reef, which is 1,240 miles long. Billions of corals created this. Bright colors and many shapes come alive in the sunlight that shines on the reef. Coral reefs are not far from land. Sunlight allows plants and animals to live there. The reef provides a nice warm home for all kinds of living things. Animals called coral form the reef. They leave the hard part of their bodies when they die. A large reef is made from many of these tiny body parts. Some coral form huge round shapes, or mounds. Some form shapes that look like animal horns.

The deep sea is very different from a coral reef. The deepest part of the ocean floor is mostly flat, but there are also mountains taller than any on land. There are valleys almost seven miles deep. The water temperature is near freezing. The weight of miles and miles of water above would easily crush a car. And yet, many types of creatures are able to live there. Huge crabs, starfish, and worms survive in the deep sea.

Ocean Life Survival

On coral reefs, animals also depend on other animals and plants to live. Small fish hide from big fish in the coral. Long and thin eels wait in the holes. They shoot out and grab a meal. Fish scrape food off the coral with their teeth. Sea grasses offer food to turtles, crabs, and fish.

GO ON →

Life on the bottom of the ocean depends on "marine snow." Tiny bits of animals and plants sink downward from above. Giant barrel sponges six feet long eat these nonliving animals and plants. Odd animals that look like flowers also feed on this snow. There is no sunlight, so green plants cannot grow there.

Will They Have the Same Fate?

The deep ocean is very different from a coral reef. Near the ocean floor, animals survive in very cold water and without sunlight. However, ocean life everywhere might be in trouble. Coral reefs are dying off. Ocean water is getting hotter. Dirt is washing into the ocean. Perhaps only the strong creatures in the deepest and most unfriendly waters will be successful and survive.

GO ON →

Name: _____ Date: _____

Now answer Numbers 6 through 10. Base your answers on "Life Underwater."

6 Read the sentence from the article.

The largest reef in the world is the <u>massive</u> Great Barrier Reef, which is 1,240 miles long.

What does the word <u>massive</u> mean in the sentence?

Ⓐ giant

Ⓑ narrow

Ⓒ rocky

Ⓓ shallow

7 Read the sentences from the article.

A large reef is made from many of these tiny body parts. Some coral form huge round shapes, or mounds. Some form shapes that look like animal horns.

What does the word <u>mounds</u> mean as it is used in the sentence?

Ⓐ fields

Ⓑ gardens

Ⓒ hills

Ⓓ holes

GO ON →

8 The author compares a coral reef to the bottom of the ocean to explain that their existence is in danger. Circle the paragraph that makes this comparison.

Ocean Life Survival

On coral reefs, animals also depend on other animals and plants to live. Small fish hide from big fish in the coral. Long and thin eels wait in the holes. They shoot out and grab a meal. Fish scrape food off the coral with their teeth. Sea grasses offer food to turtles, crabs, and fish.

Life on the bottom of the ocean depends on "marine snow." Tiny bits of animals and plants sink downward from above. Giant barrel sponges six feet long eat these nonliving animals and plants. Odd animals that look like flowers also feed on this snow. There is no sunlight, so green plants cannot grow there.

Will They Have the Same Fate?

The deep ocean is very different from a coral reef. Near the ocean floor, animals survive in very cold water and without sunlight. However, ocean life everywhere might be in trouble. Coral reefs are dying off. Ocean water is getting hotter. Dirt is washing into the ocean. Perhaps only the strong creatures in the deepest and most unfriendly waters will be successful and survive.

GO ON →

Name: _____ Date: _____

9 How are the ideas connected in the section titled "Ocean Life Survival"?

Ⓐ They list the different types of plant life.

Ⓑ They describe the landscape of the ocean.

Ⓒ They compare and contrast how sea life survives.

Ⓓ They explain how the water temperature affects sea life.

10 With which statements would the author of the article **most likely** agree? Pick **two** choices.

Ⓐ Oceans are well-protected.

Ⓑ People should care about ocean life.

Ⓒ The oceans are getting better every day.

Ⓓ Nature does not need the help of people.

Ⓔ Coral reefs are dying out around the world.

Ⓕ All sea animals are strong and able to survive.

Now answer Number 11. Base your answer on "Life in the Cold" and "Life Underwater."

11 Compare and contrast life for animals in a coral reef, at the bottom of the ocean, and in Antarctica. Include information from both articles to support your answer.

_____

_____

_____

_____

_____

_____

_____

_____

_____

_____

_____

_____

_____

Answer Key

Question	Correct Answer	Content Focus	CCSS	Complexity
1A	A	Text Structure: Compare and Contrast	RI.3.8	DOK 2
1B	D	Text Structure: Compare and Contrast/ Text Evidence	RI.3.8/ RI.3.1	DOK 2
2	D	Context Clues: Sentence Clues	L.3.4a	DOK 2
3A	D	Context Clues: Sentence Clues	L.3.4a	DOK 2
3B	A	Context Clues: Sentence Clues/ Text Evidence	L.3.4a/ RI.3.1	DOK 2
4	B, C	Text Structure: Compare and Contrast	RI.3.8	DOK 2
5	see below	Text Structure: Compare and Contrast	RI.3.8	DOK 2
6	A	Context Clues: Sentence Clues	L.3.4a	DOK 2
7	C	Context Clues: Sentence Clues	L.3.4a	DOK 2
8	see below	Text Structure: Compare and Contrast	RI.3.8	DOK 2
9	C	Text Structure: Compare and Contrast	RI.3.8	DOK 2
10	B, E	Author's Point of View	RI.3.6	DOK 3
11	see below	Writing About Text	W.3.8	DOK 4

Comprehension 2, 4, 5, 8, 9, 10	/12	%
Vocabulary 1A, 1B, 3A, 3B, 6, 7	/8	%
Total Weekly Assessment Score	/20	%

5 Students should complete the chart with the following details:
- Penguins—Have short legs; Cannot walk well
- Seals—Have thick fur; Have two sets of flippers
- Both—Have blubber; Live in Antarctica

8 Students should circle the following paragraph:
- The deep ocean is very different from a coral reef. Near the ocean floor, animals survive in very cold water and without sunlight. However, ocean life everywhere might be in trouble. Coral reefs are dying off. Ocean water is getting hotter. Dirt is washing into the ocean. Perhaps only the strong creatures in the deepest and most unfriendly waters will be successful and survive.

11 To receive full credit for the response, the following information should be included: Animals that live at the bottom of the ocean and in Antarctica can survive in very cold places. Also, the animals that live in Antarctica have blubber that protects them from the cold. Living in or near a coral reef is easier than living at the ocean bottom or in Antarctica because the reef is warm and sunny.

Read the article "Flying High" before answering Numbers 1 through 5.

Flying High

An airplane is large, long, and heavy, yet look up in the sky and you'll see planes soaring through the air. How on Earth do they ever get off the ground? And once they get off the ground, how do they stay up? If you jump up, it is only a matter of seconds before you fall back to Earth, and you are much lighter than any plane.

The answer is lift. Lift is a force that moves a plane up and holds it there. Every part of the plane helps produce lift, but the wings are the most important part. An airplane's wings are straight on the bottom but curved on the top. This shape is responsible for lifting the plane.

As a plane speeds down a runway, it is moving through air. An airplane's wings cuts through the air, forcing the air above and below it to move. The air flowing above the wing moves up and then down its curved top. As the air moves down, its speed increases. It becomes lighter. So it doesn't push down on the wing as much. Meanwhile, the heavier air under the wing's flat bottom is pushing up on the wing. Its push up is stronger than the top air's push down. So the air under the wing "wins" the game of forces. It pushes the wing up, lifting the plane off the ground.

As long as the plane keeps moving forward, the air will keep it up. On the ground, the plane's engine and wheels move it forward. Yet up in the air, wheels are no good. How does the plane move forward in the air? Its propeller helps move it forward. Each blade of a propeller is shaped like a wing. It is curved on one side and flat on the other. The curved sides face away from the plane. The flat sides face the plane. As the propeller blades spin, the air in front of them speeds up and becomes lighter. The heavier air behind the blades pushes on them, moving them forward. The plane gets pulled along for the ride.

GO ON →

How does a plane come back down safely? A pilot cannot just stop the plane from moving. The key is to slow down the air over the tops of the wings. However, the air must be slowed down gradually, little by little. So the pilot slowly cuts back on the engine. This slows down the propeller. Also, flaps on the back part of a wing can be moved so they slant up. The air moving into the flaps slows, causing it to become heavier. So it pushes down more on the wings.

Air flight is possible, then, because air can push things around. As wind, it can be strong enough to push you around. It can even be strong enough to lift a huge and heavy airplane.

Now answer Numbers 1 through 5. Base your answers on "Flying High."

1 This question has two parts. First, answer part A. Then, answer part B.

Part A: Read the paragraph. Then, answer the question.

As a plane speeds down a runway, it is moving through air. An airplane's wings cuts through the air, forcing the air above and below it to move. The air flowing above the wing moves up and then down its curved top. As the air moves down, its speed increases. It becomes lighter. So it doesn't push down on the wing as much. Meanwhile, the heavier air under the wing's flat bottom is pushing up on the wing. Its push up is stronger than the top air's push down. So the air under the wing "wins" the game of forces. It pushes the wing up, lifting the plane off the ground.

How does the author organize the ideas in the paragraph?

Ⓐ by listing the steps to land a plane

Ⓑ by comparing the speeds of different planes

Ⓒ by telling the effects air has on a plane's wings

Ⓓ by explaining the sizes of wings on different planes

Part B: Which sentence from the article **best** supports your answer in part A?

Ⓐ "As a plane speeds down a runway, it is moving through air."

Ⓑ "An airplane's wings cuts through the air, forcing the air above and below it to move."

Ⓒ "The air flowing above the wing moves up and then down its curved top."

Ⓓ "It pushes the wing up, lifting the plane off the ground."

GO ON →

2 Read the sentence from the article.

Each <u>blade</u> of a propeller is shaped like a wing.

Which meaning of the word <u>blade</u> is used in the sentence?

Ⓐ the metal part of an ice skate

Ⓑ the thin flat part of machines

Ⓒ the cutting part of a tool

Ⓓ a thin leaf of grass

3 How does the author explain how a plane moves forward? Pick **two** choices.

Ⓐ by comparing the wings of a plane to the propeller it uses

Ⓑ by listing the different types of propellers found on planes

Ⓒ by telling how a propeller works when the plane is in the air

Ⓓ by describing the different sizes of planes and how they move

Ⓔ by discussing what wheels do for the plane when it is up in the air

Ⓕ by explaining that the plane's engine and wheels move it on the ground

GO ON →

4 Read the paragraph.

How does a plane come back down safely? A pilot cannot just stop the plane from moving. The key is to slow down the air over the tops of the wings. However, the air must be slowed down gradually, little by little. So the pilot slowly cuts back on the engine. This slows down the propeller. Also, flaps on the back part of a wing can be moved so they slant up. The air moving into the flaps slows, causing it to become heavier. So it pushes down more on the wings.

How are the ideas connected in the paragraph?

Ⓐ They explain how a plane is landed.

Ⓑ They explain how the pilot stops the engine.

Ⓒ They explain why the plane becomes lighter.

Ⓓ They explain why the pilot stops the propeller.

5 The word key has different meanings. Draw a line from each sentence on the left to the correct meaning of key on the right.

The key is to slow down the air over the tops of the wings.	a button on a computer keyboard
I hit the key and sent the email to my friend.	a chart that explains symbols on a map
Use the key to find out how many miles are between the two cities.	an important or necessary thing

GO ON →

Read the article "Living in Space" before answering Numbers 6 through 10.

Living in Space

Astronauts train for many years before they go into space. They study machines and science, and they exercise to make their bodies strong. They prepare because living in space is different from living on Earth. Why?

The main reason is there is no gravity. Scientists call this state zero gravity. Without gravity, astronauts have no weight, so they float around the spaceship. Astronauts love being able to float from place to place. However, zero gravity complicates life, making things harder, like sleeping, eating, and staying healthy.

In zero gravity, astronauts go to bed in sleeping bags, but they must attach the bag to a wall or bunk bed. It's important not to float away. They might bump into something while sleeping!

A spaceship has an oven but no way to keep food cold, so there is no way to keep food from spoiling. At the beginning of a trip, astronauts can eat fresh fruit. Later they eat foods that have been dried. These are mixed with water and heated.

Astronauts can choose from many foods. They might have chicken or seafood and many kinds of vegetables. Peanut butter is plentiful. They cannot shake salt or pepper on their food, though. The salt and pepper might float away into a machine and cause a jam. They can season their food with liquid salt and pepper. All food must be stored in packages. After eating, the packages are crushed and stored to be thrown away on Earth.

Having no weight causes half of all astronauts to get space sickness. They might throw up, feel headaches, and have a hard time concentrating. Usually, astronauts feel normal again after a few days.

GO ON →

Our bodies are made mostly of water and other fluids. On Earth, gravity pulls these fluids down toward our feet. In space, the fluids travel from the legs and feet back up to the head. So in space, astronauts' faces puff up. Their legs become smaller. Astronauts also have to deal with more fluid in their noses, so they get the sniffles.

Astronauts must exercise a lot. Since gravity doesn't pull at the body, muscles grow soft. Heart muscles shrink because they have much less to do. So in space, astronauts must exercise each day. Some use a machine that works like a bicycle. Others lift weights.

Exercise helps astronauts stay strong. The stronger they are when they return to Earth, the less time it will take them to recover. Also, exercise improves astronauts' mood. It makes them feel happier.

Like people on Earth, astronauts get time off every day and on weekends. They have very stressful jobs, so relaxing is important. They might read books or watch movies. Some play video games or talk to family members. Some just gaze out the window. The Earth below gives a beautiful view!

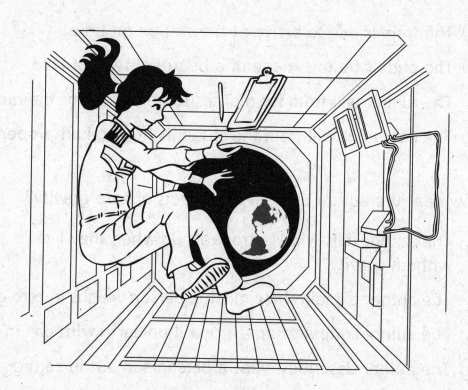

GO ON →

Name: _____ Date: _____

Now answer Numbers 6 through 10. Base your answers on "Living in Space."

6 This question has two parts. First, answer part A. Then, answer part B.

Part A: Read the sentence from the article.

Astronauts <u>train</u> for many years before they go into space.

Which meaning of the word <u>train</u> is used in the sentence?

(A) teach

(B) prepare

(C) a connected line of railway cars

(D) the part of a dress that trails behind

Part B: Which sentence uses the word <u>train</u> in the **same** way as it is used in the passage?

(A) The <u>train</u> is due to arrive at the station on time.

(B) The bride's <u>train</u> is made of a beautiful type of lace.

(C) The runner will <u>train</u> for months to get ready for the race.

(D) The instructor will <u>train</u> the students how to knit properly.

7 How does the author explain the effects of zero gravity?

(A) The author tells what astronauts do when they live without gravity.

(B) The author explains how much a person weighs in zero gravity.

(C) The author compares an astronaut on Earth with one in space.

(D) The author describes what a person can eat in zero gravity.

GO ON →

8 Read the sentence from the article.

The salt and pepper might float away into a machine and cause a jam.

Which sentence uses the word jam in the **same** way it is used in the sentence above?

(A) The band had a jam session after practice.

(B) Be careful not to jam your finger on the door.

(C) Would you like some jam with your peanut butter?

(D) The printer is not working because of a paper jam.

9 Read the paragraphs. Then, answer the question.

Our bodies are made mostly of water and other fluids. On Earth, gravity pulls these fluids down toward our feet. In space, the fluids travel from the legs and feet back up to the head. So in space, astronauts' faces puff up. Their legs become smaller. Astronauts also have to deal with more fluid in their noses, so they get the sniffles.

Astronauts must exercise a lot. Since gravity doesn't pull at the body, muscles grow soft. Heart muscles shrink because they have much less to do. So in space, astronauts must exercise each day. Some use a machine that works like a bicycle. Others lift weights.

How are the ideas in the paragraphs connected? Pick **two** choices.

(A) by comparing astronauts to athletes

(B) by telling how gravity affects our bodies

(C) by comparing life on Earth to life in space

(D) by comparing gravity to other forces in space

(E) by telling why astronauts prepare for life in space

(F) by telling how astronauts are launched into space

GO ON →

10 Complete the chart with the main idea of the article and **two** details that support the main idea. Write the correct sentences from the list. Not all sentences will be used.

Main Idea	Supporting Details

Sentences:
Exercise is necessary when in space.
Our bodies are made mostly of water.
It can be fun to float around a spaceship.
Astronauts must do things differently in space.
Astronauts must attach sleeping bags to a wall.

Name: _____ Date: _____

Now answer Number 11. Base your answer on "Flying High" and "Living in Space."

11 How do air and gravity affect airplanes and astronauts? Include information from both articles to support your answer.

_____

_____

_____

_____

_____

_____

_____

_____

_____

_____

_____

Answer Key

Name: _____

Question	Correct Answer	Content Focus	CCSS	Complexity
1A	C	Text Structure: Cause and Effect	RI.3.8	DOK 2
1B	D	Text Structure: Cause and Effect/ Text Evidence	RI.3.8/ RI.3.1	DOK 2
2	B	Multiple-Meaning Words	L.3.4a	DOK 2
3	C, F	Text Structure: Cause and Effect	RI.3.8	DOK 2
4	A	Text Structure: Cause and Effect	RI.3.8	DOK 2
5	see below	Multiple-Meaning Words	L.3.4a	DOK 2
6A	B	Multiple-Meaning Words	L.3.4a	DOK 2
6B	C	Multiple-Meaning Words/ Text Evidence	L.3.4a/ RI.3.1	DOK 2
7	A	Text Structure: Cause and Effect	RI.3.8	DOK 2
8	D	Multiple-Meaning Words	L.3.4a	DOK 2
9	B, E	Text Structure: Cause and Effect	RI.3.8	DOK 2
10	see below	Main Idea and Key Details	RI.3.2	DOK 2
11	see below	Writing About Text	W.3.8	DOK 4

Comprehension 1A, 1B, 3, 4, 7, 9, 10	/12	%
Vocabulary 2, 5, 6A, 6B, 8	/8	%
Total Weekly Assessment Score	/20	%

5 Students should make the following vocabulary matches:
- The key is to slow down the air over the tops of the wings.—an important or necessary thing
- I hit the key and sent the email to my friend.—a button on a computer keyboard
- Use the key to find out how many miles are between the two cities.—a chart that explains symbols on a map

10 Students should complete the chart as follows:
- Main Idea—Astronauts must do things differently in space.
- Supporting Details—Exercise is necessary when in space.; Astronauts must attach sleeping bags to a wall.

11 To receive full credit for the response, the following information should be included: An airplane lifts off the ground because air pushes up on its wings. An astronaut floats in a spaceship because there is no gravity and the astronaut has no weight.

Read the poem "The Assignment" before answering Numbers 1 through 5.

The Assignment

My teacher gave an assignment
I don't know where to begin
I have to write an essay
About a heroine.

She has to be a superstar
Someone I admire
A woman who's a light that guides
And sets my heart afire.

What about our mayor?
She keeps parks safe and clean
But does she take me to the store
When I need some jeans?

And there's my favorite movie star
She sings and dances too
But would she sing a lullaby
If I were only two?

I admire my music teacher, who's
A nightingale that sings
But she's never made a costume
With stars and angel wings.

GO ON →

I admire my county's senator
Her job is hard to do
She's honest and intelligent.
Can she cook brownies too?

I admire Amelia Earhart, who
Made history when she flew
But where was she the other day
When I was sick with flu?

This leads me to a conclusion
The only one to be made
I have to look quite close to home
To see who makes the grade.

A woman who's a blanket
Of love and warmth and care
Who's been with me right from the start
And always will be there.

My mom's the real rock star
My pen she will inspire
She'll be my essay's heroine cause
She's the person I admire!

GO ON →

Now answer Numbers 1 through 5. Base your answers on "The Assignment."

1 This question has two parts. First, answer part A. Then, answer part B.

Part A: Which sentence **best** describes the lesson of the poem?

(A) A heroine is someone who is a teacher.

(B) A heroine is someone who made history.

(C) A heroine is someone who is a famous rock star.

(D) A heroine is someone who does small but important things.

Part B: Which line from the poem **best** supports your answer in part A?

(A) "My teacher gave an assignment"

(B) "She has to be a superstar"

(C) "She sings and dances too"

(D) "Who's been with me right from the start"

2 The poem has a message about love and heroines. Circle the **one** message that the poem has for **each** topic.

Love	Heroines
Love is found everywhere.	Heroines are great leaders.
Love is shown in the little things you do.	Heroines do very brave things.
Love is the greatest feeling you can have.	Heroines do not have to be famous.

GO ON →

3 This question has two parts. First, answer part A. Then, answer part B.

Part A: Read the lines from the poem.

A woman who's <u>a blanket</u>
<u>Of love and warmth and care</u>

What does the phrase "a blanket of love and warmth and care" mean?

Ⓐ someone who makes blankets

Ⓑ someone who keeps the speaker warm

Ⓒ someone who takes care of the speaker

Ⓓ someone who covers the speaker with a blanket

Part B: Why does the narrator compare her heroine to a blanket?

Ⓐ to show that her heroine is comforting

Ⓑ to show that her heroine is easy to find

Ⓒ to show that her heroine is like a weight

Ⓓ to show that her heroine is soft and fuzzy

GO ON →

4 How does the speaker feel about her choice of heroine at the end of the poem? Pick **two** choices.

(A) confused

(B) nervous

(C) proud

(D) sure

(E) uncertain

(F) weary

5 Read the line from the poem.

My mom's the real rock star

Why does the speaker compare her mom to a rock star?

(A) Her mother sings and dances like a rock star.

(B) Her mother is very good at being a mom.

(C) Her mother wants to be a rock star.

(D) Her mother looks like a rock star.

GO ON →

**Read the poem "More Than Mashed Potatoes"
before answering Numbers 6 through 10.**

More Than Mashed Potatoes

I used to hate art class
'Til my teacher helped me see
That what my eyes are seeing
Are not what things can be.

Mashed potatoes aren't potatoes,
That's what he said to me.
"They're a mountain. They're a cloud.
Pour some gravy. Make a sea."

A block of wood is just that—
A piece of wood, I say.
My teacher tells me, "Look again.
Here's a tool. Go carve away."

Now a block of wood it's not,
It's a spaceship or a car.
Just remove some extra wood,
Teacher, look! I am a star!

Water paints aren't only colors,
They become just what you wish.
With some paper, brush, and water
I create a deep-sea fish.

GO ON →

Now wire's not just metal,
It's a thin man or a cat.
Make a silly face or tree
Bend it this way, or like that.

Sticks and stones, feathers, shells,
Each is much more than what you see.
And I—master cook—make art with them,
Following my recipe.

I understand art better now
Even though I'm not the smartest
There is one thing I'm certain of—
I am QUITE the artist.

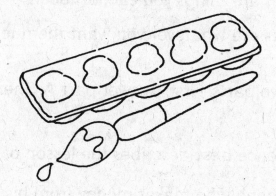

GO ON →

Name: _____ Date: _____

Now answer Numbers 6 through 10. Base your answers on "More Than Mashed Potatoes."

6 Read the stanza from the poem.

Mashed potatoes aren't potatoes,
That's what he said to me.
"They're a mountain. They're a cloud.
Pour some gravy. Make a sea."

What does the phrase "They're a mountain, They're a cloud" mean?

(A) Mashed potatoes are part of nature.

(B) Mashed potatoes are high and moist.

(C) Mashed potatoes are things you cannot touch.

(D) Mashed potatoes are whatever you want them to be.

7 This question has two parts. First, answer part A. Then, answer part B.

Part A: Which sentence **best** describes the lesson of the poem?

(A) An artist is someone who makes money from his art.

(B) An artist is anyone who uses things to make art.

(C) Art should be studied in a class.

(D) Some things are hard to see.

Part B: Which line **best** supports the lesson of the poem?

(A) "I used to hate art class"

(B) "A block of wood is just that—"

(C) "I understand art better now"

(D) "Even though I'm not the smartest"

GO ON →

8 Read the stanza from the poem.

Now a block of wood it's not,
It's a spaceship or a car.
Just remove some extra wood,
Teacher, look! I am a star!

Why does the speaker compare a block of wood to a spaceship and a car?

(A) They are the same weight.

(B) They are made of the same materials.

(C) The speaker can create a piece of art from the wood.

(D) The speaker has blocks with pictures of spaceships and cars.

9 What does the reader learn about art from reading the poem? Pick **two** choices.

(A) Unexpected materials can become art.

(B) The best type of art is made from food.

(C) Real artists use everyday objects as art.

(D) Most people are artists and they don't know it.

(E) Wood and potatoes are found in every art class.

(F) Art involves thinking about things in new ways.

GO ON →

10 Circle the stanza that **best** states the poem's message.

Now a block of wood it's not,
It's a spaceship or a car.
Just remove some extra wood,
Teacher, look! I am a star!

Water paints aren't only colors,
They become just what you wish.
With some paper, brush, and water
I create a deep-sea fish.

Now wire's not just metal,
It's a thin man or a cat.
Make a silly face or tree
Bend it this way, or like that.

Sticks and stones, feathers, shells,
Each is much more than what you see.
And I—master cook—make art with them,
Following my recipe.

I understand art better now
Even though I'm not the smartest
There is one thing I'm certain of—
I am QUITE the artist.

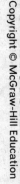

Name: _____ Date: _____

Now answer Number 11. Base your answer on "The Assignment" and "More Than Mashed Potatoes."

11 What do the speakers of both poems discover about people and objects in their everyday lives? Include details from both poems to support your answer.

_____

_____

_____

_____

_____

_____

_____

_____

_____

_____

_____

_____

Answer Key

Name: _____

Question	Correct Answer	Content Focus	CCSS	Complexity
1A	D	Theme	RL.3.2	DOK 3
1B	D	Theme/Text Evidence	RL.3.2/ RL.3.1	DOK 3
2	see below	Theme	RL.3.2	DOK 3
3A	C	Figurative Language: Metaphors	RL.3.4	DOK 2
3B	A	Figurative Language: Metaphors/ Text Evidence	RL.3.4/ RL.3.1	DOK 2
4	C, D	Point of View	RL.3.6	DOK 3
5	B	Figurative Language: Metaphors	RL.3.4	DOK 2
6	D	Figurative Language: Metaphors	RL.3.4	DOK 2
7A	B	Theme	RL.3.2	DOK 3
7B	C	Theme/Text Evidence	RL.3.2/ RL.3.1	DOK 3
8	C	Figurative Language: Metaphors	RL.3.4	DOK 2
9	A, F	Theme	RL.3.2	DOK 3
10	see below	Theme	RL.3.2	DOK 3
11	see below	Writing About Text	W.3.8	DOK 4

Comprehension 1A, 1B, 2, 4, 7A, 7B, 9, 10	/12	%
Vocabulary 3A, 3B, 5, 6, 8	/8	%
Total Weekly Assessment Score	/20	%

2 Students should circle the following statements:
- Love—Love is shown in the little things you do.
- Heroines—Heroines do not have to be famous.

10 Students should circle the following stanza:
- I understand art better now
  Even though I'm not the smartest
  There is one thing I'm certain of—
  I am QUITE the artist.

11 To receive full credit for the response, the following information should be included: The speaker in "The Assignment" decides that her mother is a heroine. The speaker in "More Than Mashed Potatoes" discovers that things like potatoes and wood can become art and that anyone can be an artist.

Read the passage "The Shelter Dogs" before answering Numbers 1 through 5.

The Shelter Dogs

I wanted a dog for as long as I could remember, and finally my dream was coming true. I was getting a puppy!

My parents and my little brother Sam and I went to the dog shelter. There were many dogs there, but my eyes were immediately drawn to a little golden puppy. I ran over to the kennel door and put my hand through the wire. The puppy looked up at me with its big brown eyes, and it lovingly licked my fingers, making my heart melt.

Sam ran over to the kennel and squealed, "This is a really cute one, Alise!"

Charlie, the man who ran the shelter said, "That is Sandy, a Labrador retriever and an excellent choice. The dog owner couldn't handle all that energy, so he brought the puppy to us. Of course, we have a variety of other dogs, too."

"No, this one," Sam and I said together, so Charlie lifted Sandy out of the kennel and handed her to me to pet. Sam wanted his turn, so I passed Sandy to Sam, who rubbed his face into the dog's fur and lovingly stroked it with his hands. Then, moments later, Sam began to sneeze violently. He rubbed his eyes, and they began to water and turn red.

Then Dad said the words no one wanted to hear: "I believe Sam is allergic to dogs!"

Now I was crying, but it wasn't because I had allergies. I wanted a dog, and I wanted that dog.

We slowly walked out of the shelter, and then Charlie stopped us. He looked at me and said, "You know, we need volunteers here, Alise. If you have an hour or so every other day, we could use your help."

GO ON →

Dad and Mom nodded. I didn't need any more encouragement, so I said, "I'll be here tomorrow!"

So every other day Mom took me to the shelter to work, although it was more fun than work. I played with the puppies, and I fed and exercised them. I began to train Sandy to sit and come when called. Charlie said that I had a great way with dogs.

Then one day, Sandy was gone. She had been adopted. I was happy for her, but I still fought back tears. Then Charlie took me to a curly-haired dog that had just come into the shelter. It was about six months old, blonde, and had big brown eyes. "This is Ginger," he said as I kneeled down to pet her. She was very playful and ran to the corner of the kennel to bring me a toy. She was just as cute as Sandy, and maybe a little smarter!

Then Charlie said, "Let's go outside. I have a surprise for you." Charlie put a leash on Ginger and we walked outside. Waiting for us was my family, including Sam!

Charlie said, "Sam, meet Ginger. She's a different breed of dog that won't make you sneeze because she's allergy-free."

Sam hesitated, but Mom told him to go ahead and touch Ginger. He did, and Ginger wagged her tail and licked his face. He hugged her and waited, but nothing happened!

So that's how we got a dog. She's half poodle and half Labrador retriever, and neither half makes Sam sick!

GO ON →

Name: _____ Date: _____

Now answer Numbers 1 through 5. Base your answers on "The Shelter Dogs."

1 This question has two parts. First, answer part A. Then, answer part B.

Part A: Who is the narrator of the passage?

Ⓐ Sam

Ⓑ Alise

Ⓒ Charlie

Ⓓ Alise's father

Part B: Which sentence from the passage **best** supports your answer in part A?

Ⓐ "I was getting a puppy!"

Ⓑ "I ran over to the kennel door and put my hand through the wire."

Ⓒ "He looked at me and said, 'You know, we need volunteers here, Alise.'"

Ⓓ "'This is Ginger,' he said as I kneeled down to pet her."

2 Read the sentence from the passage.

The puppy looked up at me with its big brown eyes, and it lovingly licked my fingers, making my heart melt.

What does lovingly **most likely** mean?

Ⓐ with joy

Ⓑ with sadness

Ⓒ with a gentle feeling

Ⓓ with an angry feeling

GO ON →

3 Arrange the events from the passage in the correct sequence. Write the sentences in the correct order in the chart below.

1	
2	
3	
4	

Events:

Dad says that Sam is allergic to dogs.

The family decides to get a puppy.

Sam puts his face in Sandy's fur.

Alise finds Sandy and pets her.

GO ON →

4 This question has two parts. First, answer part A. Then, answer part B.

Part A: Read the paragraph from the passage.

Dad and Mom nodded. I didn't need any more <u>encouragement</u>, so I said, "I'll be here tomorrow!"

What does the word <u>encouragement</u> **most likely** mean?

(A) work

(B) happiness

(C) help or support

(D) questions and answers

Part B: What is the root word of <u>encouragement</u>?

(A) age

(B) courage

(C) enable

(D) rage

5 What does the point of view in the passage help to explain? Pick **two** choices.

(A) why Sam begins to sneeze

(B) why Alise decides to volunteer

(C) how Alise feels about getting a dog

(D) how the parents feel about the dogs

(E) how the dogs feel about Alise and Sam

(F) why Charlie asks for help at the shelter

GO ON →

Read the passage "Family Meetings" before answering Numbers 6 through 10.

Family Meetings

Tyrone hated family meetings. Before their meeting, his parents tried to make him feel at ease by making his favorite food, ham and cheese sandwiches. Then they talked to him and his brother, Darnell, about doing something they didn't want to do. Tyrone's mother started the meeting, but he couldn't hear what she was saying very well. His baby sister, Keisha, was screaming and making her usual racket.

"The whole family is moving," his mom announced. "Keisha is leaving our bedroom and will be moving into Darnell's room. Darnell will be moving into Tyrone's room."

"No way!" Tyrone screamed. His stomach felt like a cement mixer. "He's got ten million plastic models all over the place for decoration and I am a neat freak. I can't work comfortably if my desktop and dresser aren't totally clear."

"Okay, here's how we will do this," Darnell said. "We'll put a line of tape down the middle of the room so that you get your side and I get mine. I'll hang my models from the ceiling, but I get to paint my side of the room blue, and I get to paint the ceiling blue too!"

Tyrone hated blue. "You can't pick the color. It's my room, too! And you got the whole ceiling!"

Their father held up his hands. "I have a compromise. You guys both love your flag football team. The team colors are blue and green. What if you both paint stripes of blue and green all over the walls?"

GO ON →

Tyrone wasn't so sure he liked this, but the next day they started painting. He secretly had to admit that painting the room was fun. He and his brother were having a wild celebration. Green stripes swirled around the walls from floor to ceiling. A gigantic blue stripe flowed like a river down Darnell's wall.

Their mother wanted to give the room a completely new appearance. "Let's put down a green carpet on the floor," she suggested, "and I'll paint clouds on the blue ceiling so it will be like there's no ceiling at all!"

Tyrone wanted his desk to stay in front of the window. It mattered to him that he could see the yard while he did homework. Darnell wanted his desk in front of the window, too. Their mother moved the desks face to face with a bookcase between them. That way they could both look out the window and not have to stare at each other while they worked.

In the end, out came the ham and cheese sandwiches again for family meetings. Tyrone decided that they should have their meetings in his—he had to stop himself—their room. He laid down beside his mom and dad on the soft floor with Keisha between them. They looked up at the beautiful clouds and the airplane models flying overhead. Oh, it was an unfortunate fact that Darnell was there too, but Tyrone just loved family meetings now.

GO ON →

Name: _____ Date: _____

Now answer Numbers 6 through 10. Base your answers on "Family Meetings."

6 This question has two parts. First, answer part A. Then, answer part B.

Part A: What does Tyrone think about sharing a room with Darnell at the beginning of the passage?

(A) He does not want to share with Darnell.

(B) He does not think Darnell will do it.

(C) He thinks it is a funny joke.

(D) He thinks it is a good idea.

Part B: Which detail from the passage **best** supports your answer in part A?

(A) "Tyrone hated family meetings."

(B) "His baby sister, Keisha, was screaming . . ."

(C) "'The whole family is moving,' his mom announced."

(D) "'No way!' Tyrone screamed."

7 Read the sentence from the passage.

Their mother wanted to give the room a completely new <u>appearance</u>.

The root word *appear* means "to be seen." What does the word <u>appearance</u> **most likely** mean?

(A) the way something looks

(B) the way something smells

(C) the way something is built

(D) the way something has changed

GO ON →

Name: _____ Date: _____

8 Choose **one** word to describe Tyrone's point of view as he paints the room with Darnell. Then choose **one** sentence from the passage that supports the point of view. Write your choices in the chart.

Tyrone's Point of View	Text Evidence

Point of View:
angry
excited
confused
thankful

Text Evidence:
"He and his brother were having a wild celebration."
"Green stripes swirled around the walls from floor to ceiling."
"A gigantic blue stripe flowed like a river down Darnell's wall."
"Tyrone wanted his desk to stay in front of the window."

GO ON →

9 How does Tyrone feel at the end of the story? Pick **two** choices.

(A) He is proud of his new room.

(B) He begins to like flag football.

(C) He begins to like the color blue.

(D) He begins to like family meetings.

(E) He is surprised about sharing a room.

(F) He is happy his sister has her own room.

10 This question has two parts. First, answer part A. Then, answer part B.

Part A: Read the detail from the passage.

Oh, it was an <u>unfortunate</u> fact that Darnell was there too, . . .

What does the word unfortunate **most likely** mean?

(A) not bad

(B) not real

(C) not long

(D) not lucky

Part B: Which other word has the same root word as unfortunate?

(A) forty

(B) fortunately

(C) tunnel

(D) unforgettable

**Now answer Number 11. Base your answer on "The Shelter Dogs"
and "Family Meetings."**

11 How do the characters in both passages find a way to get what
they want and still make everyone happy? Include details from
both passages to support your answer.

_____

_____

_____

_____

_____

_____

_____

_____

_____

_____

_____

_____

Answer Key

Name: _____

Question	Correct Answer	Content Focus	CCSS	Complexity
1A	B	Point of View	RL.3.6	DOK 2
1B	C	Point of View/Text Evidence	RL.3.6/ RL.3.1	DOK 2
2	C	Root Words	L.3.4c	DOK 1
3	see below	Character, Setting, Plot: Sequence	RL.3.3	DOK 1
4A	C	Root Words	L.3.4c	DOK 1
4B	B	Root Words/Text Evidence	L.3.4c/ RL.3.1	DOK 1
5	B, C	Point of View	RL.3.6	DOK 3
6A	A	Point of View	RL.3.6	DOK 3
6B	D	Point of View/Text Evidence	RL.3.6/ RL.3.1	DOK 3
7	A	Root Words	L.3.4c	DOK 1
8	see below	Point of View	RL.3.6	DOK 3
9	A, D	Point of View	RL.3.6	DOK 3
10A	D	Root Words	L.3.4c	DOK 1
10B	B	Root Words/Text Evidence	L.3.4c/ RL.3.1	DOK 1
11	see below	Writing About Text	W.3.8	DOK 4

Comprehension 1A, 1B, 3, 5, 6A, 6B, 8, 9	/12	%
Vocabulary 2, 4A, 4B, 7, 10A, 10B	/8	%
Total Weekly Assessment Score	/20	%

3 Students should put the events in the following order:
- 1—The family decides to get a puppy.
- 2—Alise finds Sandy and pets her.
- 3—Sam puts his face in Sandy's fur.
- 4—Dad says that Sam is allergic to dogs.

8 Students should complete the chart with the following details:
- Point of View—excited
- Text Evidence—"He and his brother were having a wild celebration."

11 To receive full credit for the response, the following information should be included: Both characters learn to compromise to get what they want. Alise learns how to take care of a dog and get one that everyone can be happy with. Tyrone learns to share his room with his brother and agree on the best way to decorate their room.

Read the passage "The Drum Set" before answering Numbers 1 through 5.

The Drum Set

Gabe used everything around him as a drum. He beat on the sofa. Bum-de-bum-de-bum! Boom! He beat on his school desk. He even pounded on his knees. His life was a steady beat of drum sounds.

All Gabe wanted was a drum set, but his parents couldn't afford to buy him one. Then, one day at school, his class began studying the importance of ecology. Mr. Gomez said that we need to protect Earth and its resources, and then he named three things that everyone could do to help protect Earth: reduce, reuse, and recycle.

As Mr. Gomez spoke, Gabe thought about what he and his family did. They recycled bottles, cans, paper, plastic, and cardboard. They didn't waste a lot, either. Gabe's new jackets were never actually new because his older and bigger brother had worn them years before. They also reduced what they used. They turned off lights when they could and reduced the amount of heat in their house at night when they were asleep.

As Mr. Gomez spoke, Gabe began to think about things he could recycle and reuse. Then a brilliant idea hit him. Not only could he help protect Earth, but he could also do something to make himself very happy! Then Mr. Gomez told the class they had to do a science project. By this time, Gabe didn't need any more encouragement. He already knew what he would do.

GO ON →

He gathered his materials. He found some big balloons left over from his birthday party. Next he searched for recycling materials and found old tin cans of different sizes including an old soup can, a large tomato can, and a huge peach can. Then he borrowed some thick tape from his father. He cut off the narrow end of each balloon and stretched a balloon over the top of each can. To seal the balloon on the can, he taped the balloon on the side of the can.

He found a set of old chopsticks and tried out his drums. The large peach can made a low sound and the tomato can made a very loud sound, while the smallest can made a higher sound. Then he began drumming with the wooden chopsticks. He sounded pretty good!

The science presentations were held on Monday. When it was Gabe's turn, he took out his drums and began playing. When he finished his performance, his classmates clapped and clapped. He was a big hit!

Then everyone looked at the doorway. The principal, Mrs. Lazek, was standing there and said, "Gabe, you've got some talent."

Gabe blushed, but Mrs. Lazek didn't give him time to answer. She continued, "We are starting a school band and have just ordered a set of drums. Would you be interested in playing the drums for our band?"

Gabe was speechless, but he swallowed and muttered, "Yes, ma'am."

"Excellent," she said. "So you'll start next Monday after school. I'll see you there!"

GO ON →

Name: _____ Date: _____

Now answer Numbers 1 through 5. Base your answers on "The Drum Set."

1 This question has two parts. First, answer part A. Then, answer part B.

Part A: Who is telling the story?

(A) Gabe

(B) Gabe's dad

(C) Gabe's mom

(D) an outside narrator

Part B: Which sentence from the passage **best** supports your answer in part A?

(A) "All Gabe wanted was a drum set, but his parents couldn't afford to buy him one."

(B) "Then, one day at school, his class began studying the importance of ecology."

(C) "The science presentations were held on Monday."

(D) "Then everyone looked at the doorway."

2 Read the sentences from the passage.

He <u>beat</u> on the sofa. Bum-de-bum-de-bum! Boom!

Which definition of the word <u>beat</u> is used in the sentences?

(A) to win against

(B) to mix by stirring

(C) to hit again and again

(D) to arrive before someone else

GO ON →

3 Read the sentences from the passage.

They recycled bottles, cans, paper, plastic, and cardboard. They didn't waste a lot, either.

Which word from the sentences means "to make poor use of something" and can also mean "unwanted materials"?

(A) recycled

(B) cans

(C) cardboard

(D) waste

4 Which inferences can you make about Gabe based on the details about how he makes the recycled drums? Pick **two** choices.

(A) He does not like to recycle.

(B) He cares about saving Earth.

(C) He does not like Mr. Gomez's class.

(D) He wants to teach his family to recycle.

(E) He thinks of ways to solve his problems.

(F) He needs to practice playing the drums.

GO ON →

5 Draw a line to match the part of the story on the left with details on the right that show how Gabe feels.

Part of Story	**How Gabe Feels**
Beginning	Excited to start working on his idea
When Mr. Gomez talks about ecology	Anxious to get what he wants
When Mr. Gomez gives a new project	Embarrassed because he is praised in front of the whole class
End	Interested as he begins to think of a new idea

GO ON →

Read the passage "The Art Show" before answering Numbers 6 through 10.

The Art Show

I really didn't know Miss Gertie at all. She was our neighbor, but she mostly kept to herself, and to be truthful, I didn't really want to know her. I never saw her smile, and I often saw her talking to the ground. Also, there was a dense stand of pine trees behind her house. It was as if she had her own personal forest. Then about a month ago, I accidentally kicked my soccer ball into her yard. I sneaked past the boundary line that separated our yards, walked to the edge of the trees, and grabbed the ball.

"You'll do very nicely," a voice said.

I jumped like a scared rabbit. There was Miss Gertie, but she wasn't talking about me—she was talking to a heap of some pebbles! She picked them up and placed them at the base of a tree trunk. I blinked, not believing my eyes. Below the tree stood a tiny house made of sticks, bark, and moss. The pebbles had become a walkway to the front of the house!

"Young man, do you like my little houses?" Miss Gertie asked. She seemed to be speaking to me, but I couldn't tell because she was not looking at me.

"Yes, ma'am," I heard myself say. Then she motioned for me to follow her. She led me through her tiny forest that was less scary than just plain amazing. There were dozens of houses scattered along a wooded pathway, all with walkways, chimneys, and even woodpiles.

"This is wonderful. I figure there are at least fifty of these," I heard myself say. And then, Miss Gertie looked directly at me and gave me the biggest smile ever.

"You have to share this," I said.

GO ON →

"Oh, no," she said and her smile disappeared. "People will laugh at me."

"No, they won't," I insisted. "This will help them appreciate nature." Then a brilliant idea hit me. "I know! We can have an art show in your backyard!"

"But is this art?" Miss Gertie asked.

"Of course it is, and we can help them make these little houses, too."

So we began to plan our outdoor art gallery. For the next few weeks, we gathered outdoor materials and made fliers and posters to advertise the art show. The day before the show, we put balloons out in front of the house and placed arrows on signs along the path that led to each little house.

The day of the show, Miss Gertie was nervous because she thought no one would come. "Patience," I said, and at that moment, a few kids from the neighborhood showed up. Fifteen minutes later, there were about fifty people tiptoeing among the little houses!

Miss Gertie set up a long table where people could build their own little houses, and carefully, she showed each child how to form the outline of a house. There was a crowd of kids of all ages making the houses with sticks, bark, glue, and acorns. An hour after the show started, a local newspaper reporter came and took pictures.

At the end of the day, Miss Gertie and I were tired, but we had done an amazing thing. We shared the beauty of nature and art, and now there would be little houses all over the neighborhood.

GO ON →

Now answer Numbers 6 through 10. Base your answers on "The Art Show."

6 This question has two parts. First, answer part A. Then, answer part B.

Part A: What does the narrator think of Miss Gertie at the beginning of the story?

(A) She is a successful artist.

(B) She is an unusual person.

(C) She is helpful in the community.

(D) She is mean to people in the neighborhood.

Part B: Which sentence from the passage **best** supports your answer in part A?

(A) "I really didn't know Miss Gertie at all."

(B) "I never saw her smile, and I often saw her talking to the ground."

(C) "Also, there was a dense stand of pine trees behind her house."

(D) "It was as if she had her own personal forest."

GO ON →

7 Read the sentence from the passage.

There was Miss Gertie, but she wasn't talking about me—she was talking to a <u>heap</u> of some pebbles!

What does the word <u>heap</u> mean in the sentence?

Ⓐ a pile

Ⓑ to give

Ⓒ to put on top

Ⓓ a huge amount

8 Which events happen **after** the narrator discovers the little houses? Pick **two** choices.

Ⓐ Miss Gertie speaks to the pebbles.

Ⓑ Miss Gertie speaks to the narrator.

Ⓒ The narrator counts the many houses.

Ⓓ The narrator gets the idea for the art show.

Ⓔ Miss Gertie begins to build things in her yard.

Ⓕ The narrator kicks the ball into Miss Gertie's yard.

9 Underline the word in the paragraph that can mean "the shape of something" or "a numeral."

"This is wonderful. I figure there are at least fifty of these," I heard myself say. And then, Miss Gertie looked directly at me and gave me the biggest smile ever.

GO ON →

10 This question has two parts. First, answer part A. Then, answer part B.

Part A: Which sentence **best** explains how the narrator feels about Miss Gertie at the end of the passage?

(A) The narrator thinks Miss Gertie is grumpy.

(B) The narrator thinks Miss Gertie talks too much.

(C) The narrator thinks Miss Gertie is a talented artist.

(D) The narrator thinks Miss Gertie should smile more often.

Part B: Which sentence from the passage **best** supports your answer in part A?

(A) "There was a crowd of kids of all ages making the houses with sticks, bark, glue, and acorns."

(B) "An hour after the show started, a local newspaper reporter came and took pictures."

(C) "At the end of the day, Miss Gertie and I were tired, but we had done an amazing thing."

(D) "We shared the beauty of nature and art, and now there would be little houses all over the neighborhood."

Weekly Assessment · Unit 5, Week 2

Name: _____ Date: _____

Now answer Number 11. Base your answer on "The Drum Set" and "The Art Show."

11 How do the main characters in "The Drum Set" and "The Art Show" feel about nature and Earth's resources? Include details from both passages to support your answer.

_____

_____

_____

_____

_____

_____

_____

_____

_____

_____

_____

_____

Answer Key

Name: _____

Question	Correct Answer	Content Focus	CCSS	Complexity
1A	D	Point of View	RL.3.6	DOK 2
1B	A	Point of View/Text Evidence	RL.3.6/ RL.3.1	DOK 2
2	C	Homographs	L.3.4a	DOK 1
3	D	Homographs	L.3.4a	DOK 1
4	B, E	Point of View	RL.3.6	DOK 3
5	see below	Point of View	RL.3.6	DOK 3
6A	B	Point of View	RL.3.6	DOK 3
6B	B	Point of View/Text Evidence	RL.3.6/ RL.3.1	DOK 3
7	A	Homographs	L.3.4a	DOK 1
8	C, D	Character, Setting, Plot: Sequence	RL.3.3	DOK 1
9	see below	Homographs	L.3.4a	DOK 1
10A	C	Point of View	RL.3.6	DOK 3
10B	D	Point of View/Text Evidence	RL.3.6/ RL.3.1	DOK 3
11	see below	Writing About Text	W.3.8	DOK 4

Comprehension 1A, 1B, 4, 5, 6A, 6B, 8, 10A, 10B		/12	%
Vocabulary 2, 3, 7, 9		/8	%
Total Weekly Assessment Score		/20	%

5 Students should make the following matches between the part of the story and Gabe's point of view:
- Beginning—Anxious to get what he wants
- When Mr. Gomez talks about ecology—Interested as he begins to think of a new idea
- When Mr. Gomez gives a new project—Excited to start working on his idea
- End—Embarrassed because he is praised in front of the whole class

9 Students should underline the word "figure" in the paragraph.

11 To receive full credit for the response, the following information should be included: Gabe in "The Drum Set" cares about Earth because he reuses and recycles materials to make his drums. The narrator in "The Art Show" tells Miss Gertie that she should share her art so others can appreciate nature and how she used materials found in nature to create her little houses.

Read the article "K–9 Search and Rescue Dogs" before answering Numbers 1 through 5.

K-9 Search and Rescue Dogs

If you ever saw an eight-week-old Australian shepherd, you would probably faint. You would squeal, "That's the cutest puppy in the world!" You would want to pick him up and pet his silky little ears and rub his soft little tummy. Your parents might let you take him home. You would care for him by teaching him rules to follow, but best of all, you would play with him.

Gradually, he would recognize his name. He would follow commands like "Sit!" and "Roll over!" and dart quickly after a ball. With some coaxing and encouraging, he might find his favorite toy hidden in the leaves. Then, you would give him treats, and in the end, you would have a wonderful pet. The professional word for cuddling and playing with your puppy is "socialization."

K–9 search and rescue team dogs are trained in these ways, but they are also given extra training by their handlers. Together, they solve crimes and save lives. Many of these dogs are rescued from shelters. Others are raised from the time they are puppies to do this special job. Their training is serious business. It is a challenge to finish it. Hard work is required for both the dog and its handler.

Dogs can do work that humans cannot do. Because of their incredible sense of smell, they have long been used to find lost people. They are also small enough to squeeze into tight places like ruined buildings.

These dogs have to be calm around humans. They have to obey their handlers in dangerous situations. Fetching a ball is another step in the training process. It teaches a dog to find something that is lost. The treats tell the dog he is doing a great job!

GO ON →

You have probably seen dogs sweeping their heads back and forth. Their noses spread open to pick up scents. This is called "air-scenting." Other dogs do "ground-scenting." They sweep their noses along the ground to find a scent their handler gave them. A piece of clothing from a missing person is all a dog needs. It will follow tiny clues left behind. Dogs also have the ability to do "odor-layering." They can pick out and follow dozens of different smells. In the same air humans would only smell one or two things. This helps in a disaster like an earthquake. Dogs use their noses to sniff out trapped victims and find people deep in the foundation of a fallen building.

K–9 teams also work with fire departments. These skilled dogs are amazing. They are trained to smell traces of fuels like gasoline. They can help find the cause of a fire. This helps firefighters tell if it was started on purpose. These brave dogs also help find people trapped inside burning buildings.

The next time you see a cute puppy, don't just pet him. Think about all the extraordinary and unusual ways dogs help humans. They are truly our best friends.

GO ON →

Name: _____ Date: _____

Now answer Numbers 1 through 5. Base your answers on "K–9 Search and Rescue Dogs."

1 This question has two parts. First, answer part A. Then, answer part B.

Part A: Read the sentence from the article.

The professional word for cuddling and playing with your puppy is "socialization."

What does the word socialization suggest about the puppy?

Ⓐ It is getting used to walking.

Ⓑ It is learning how to help people.

Ⓒ It is learning how to act like a dog.

Ⓓ It is getting used to being with people.

Part B: Which word from the sentence **best** supports your answer in part A?

Ⓐ professional

Ⓑ word

Ⓒ playing

Ⓓ puppy

GO ON →

2 Which statements describe the author's view about regular dog training? Pick **two** choices.

(A) It is not necessary for every dog.

(B) It will make dogs into wonderful pets.

(C) It will result in a search and rescue dog.

(D) It will help people enjoy their dogs more.

(E) It is not done that often by most dog owners.

(F) It will be difficult because dogs do not listen well.

3 This question has two parts. First, answer part A. Then, answer part B.

Part A: How does the author feel about the training of a search and rescue dog?

(A) It is not always worth it.

(B) It is not easy to complete.

(C) It takes less time than people think.

(D) It takes the help of many people and dogs.

Part B: Which sentence from the article **best** supports your answer in part A?

(A) "Together, they solve crimes and save lives."

(B) "Many of these dogs are rescued from shelters."

(C) "Hard work is required for both the dog and its handler."

(D) "Dogs can do work that humans cannot do."

GO ON →

4 Read the sentence from the article.

Dogs use their noses to sniff out trapped victims and find people deep in the <u>foundation</u> of a fallen building.

What does the word <u>foundation</u> **most likely** mean?

(A) attic

(B) basement

(C) porch

(D) rooftop

5 Choose the sentences that show the author's point of view about dogs. Write **two** sentences in the chart.

Author's Point of View About Dogs

Sentences:
All dogs can become K–9 dogs.
Handlers do not always like dogs.
Dog have the same skills as people.
People should have fun with their dogs.
K–9 dogs are often not very well-behaved.
Dogs can do many things that people cannot.

GO ON →

Read the article "The Ideal Basketball Team" before answering Numbers 6 through 10.

The Ideal Basketball Team

Most people think a basketball team needs one tall player to score all the points. It never hurts to have a superstar, but the great teams succeed because they have a variety of different players.

Only five players from each team are allowed on the court at a time. Each of these teammates has a role and is expected to know what to do. Different players have different talents. A good team works together, and all these talents come together at just the right moment.

Teams do need at least one tall player. This player rebounds the ball, which involves grabbing the ball when someone misses a shot. Without tall players, or a big jumper, the other team will get all the rebounds. This tall player is usually the center. He is called that because this player roams around in the center near the basket.

The next key player is a ball handler and passer called a point guard. The point guard has a big job that involves the responsibility of controlling the game. He must dribble well. No one can take the ball away from this ball handler. Another player is the guard. He plays far from the basket and passes the ball to players near the net.

The two other players are shooters. They can be a guard who shoots long shots or a player who is taller and plays closer to the basket. He is called a forward. His job is to put the ball in the basket. Forwards usually make half of the shots they attempt. They are fast and tremendous jumpers who can also dribble well. They move easily to the basket to get easier shots.

Copyright © McGraw-Hill Education

GO ON →

Some of the best professional and college basketball teams win almost every game they play. Not only do they have great players in every position, but they also play good defense. They have stars, but the players work together. They put on a brilliant show every night. They make winning look easy because of their great talents.

Every position on a team is hard. A huge center may tower over everyone else, but he gets hit a lot under the basket. Quick guards have to run fast throughout the game and get open to shoot. Forwards have to do a little of what guards and centers do. On the best basketball teams, the players on the court can play any position and they all work well together.

GO ON →

Now answer Numbers 6 through 10. Base your answers on "The Ideal Basketball Team."

6 This question has two parts. First, answer part A. Then, answer part B.

Part A: Which sentence **best** describes the main idea of the article?

Ⓐ One player has to shoot the ball well and score.

Ⓑ Each player on the court has only one job to do.

Ⓒ A good basketball team plays together and wins.

Ⓓ Most basketball teams have only five good players.

Part B: Which sentence from the article **best** states the main idea?

Ⓐ "Most people think a basketball team needs one tall player to score all the points."

Ⓑ "A good team works together, and all these talents come together at just the right moment."

Ⓒ "Without tall players, or a big jumper, the other team will get all the rebounds."

Ⓓ "They make winning look easy because of their great talents."

7 Circle the word in the sentence that **best** helps to explain the meaning of responsibility.

The point guard has a big job that involves the responsibility of controlling the game.

GO ON →

8 With which statements would the author **most likely** agree? Pick **two** choices.

(A) It helps to be tall when playing basketball.

(B) It takes years to learn how to play basketball.

(C) Basketball is a good example of a team sport.

(D) It is more fun to watch basketball than to play it.

(E) Basketball players should learn their position only.

(F) Basketball is more fun to play than any other sport.

9 Which text evidence **best** shows the author's point of view that basketball is a difficult game to play?

(A) "Different players have different talents."

(B) "This tall player is usually the center."

(C) "The two other players are shooters."

(D) "Every position on a team is hard."

GO ON →

10 This question has two parts. First, answer part A. Then, answer part B.

Part A: Read the sentences from the article.

Forwards usually make half of the shots they attempt. They are fast and tremendous jumpers who can also dribble well.

What does the word tremendous **most likely** mean?

(A) clever

(B) fantastic

(C) ordinary

(D) slow

Part B: Which word from the sentences **best** helps you understand the meaning of tremendous?

(A) forwards

(B) attempt

(C) fast

(D) dribble

Now answer Number 11. Base your answer on "K–9 Search and Rescue Dogs" and "The Ideal Basketball Team."

11 In each article, the author talks about special talents. What are the special talents of a rescue dog? What are the special talents of a good basketball player? How do both use their special talents to succeed? Include information from both articles to support your answer.

_____

_____

_____

_____

_____

_____

_____

_____

_____

_____

_____

_____

Answer Key

Question	Correct Answer	Content Focus	CCSS	Complexity
1A	D	Context Clues: Sentence Clues	L.3.4a	DOK 2
1B	C	Context Clues: Sentence Clues/ Text Evidence	L.3.4a/ RI.3.1	DOK 2
2	B, D	Author's Point of View	RI.3.6	DOK 3
3A	B	Author's Point of View	RI.3.6	DOK 3
3B	C	Author's Point of View/ Text Evidence	RI.3.6/ RI.3.1	DOK 3
4	B	Context Clues: Sentence Clues	L.3.4a	DOK 2
5	see below	Author's Point of View	RI.3.6	DOK 3
6A	C	Main Idea and Key Details	RI.3.2	DOK 2
6B	B	Main Idea and Key Details/ Text Evidence	RI.3.2/ RI.3.1	DOK 2
7	see below	Context Clues: Sentence Clues	L.3.4a	DOK 1
8	A, C	Author's Point of View	RI.3.6	DOK 3
9	D	Author's Point of View	RI.3.6	DOK 3
10A	B	Context Clues: Sentence Clues	L.3.4a	DOK 2
10B	C	Context Clues: Sentence Clues/ Text Evidence	L.3.4a/ RI.3.1	DOK 2
11	see below	Writing About Text	W.3.8	DOK 4

Comprehension 2, 3A, 3B, 5, 6A, 6B, 8, 9		/12	%
Vocabulary 1A, 1B, 4, 7, 10A, 10B		/8	%
Total Weekly Assessment Score		/20	%

5 Students should complete the chart with the following sentences:
- People should have fun with their dogs.
- Dogs can do many things that people cannot.

7 Students should circle the word "job" in the sentence.

11 To receive full credit for the response, the following information should be included: Special talents of a rescue dog include a good sense of smell and calmness in dangerous situations. Special talents of a good basketball player include the ability to play multiple positions and to work with others on a team. A rescue dog can help people in dangerous situations and a good basketball player can work with his team to win the game.

Read the letter to the editor "Let's Lose the Litter" before answering Numbers 1 through 5.

Let's Lose the Litter

Dear Editor:

Take one look around our city. You will see fine buildings, lovely parks, and busy streets. You will also see papers, cans, plastic bags, and other sorts of trash. Litter blows about in the breeze. It collects in gutters, and it gets snared by branches and bushes. Last week I saw fast-food wrappers floating on the duck pond in Central Park. This is what happens when trash is improperly thrown away. Our city has a litter problem, and we must do something about it.

We need to start a city program to clean up the litter. People have joined together in other places to pick up litter. One group called the Trash Masters picks up trash along its island's roads. In many areas company workers or members of social groups promise to be cleanup volunteers. They regularly pick up and bag litter along sections of highways. These cleanup programs have been successful elsewhere, so one can be successful in our city.

Litter is ugly, which is enough to make it unacceptable, but it has far worse effects than just ugliness. Litter can dirty our water and harm wildlife and the places where animals live. It can cause health problems. It also costs time and money to clean up.

GO ON →

That is why we should not just clean up litter. We should also keep people from littering in the first place. It can start with each of us. We can set an example by throwing our trash away properly. The city must provide enough trash cans along streets and in parks.

The next step is to teach people not to litter. Cities around the country have "Don't Litter" programs. In Austin, Texas, it is called "Let's Can It." In Philadelphia, they say "UnLitter Us." Posters around these cities tell people not to litter. They show the ugly effects of littering. In Missouri, school kids won a trash can decorating contest. They decorated their trash can like a spaceship. Then they added the sign "Blast Trash Out of This World." Our city can start a "Don't Litter" program, too. It can teach people not to litter and it can also be fun.

We must begin today. Stopping litter is not an unreachable goal. If we are unsuccessful in stopping litter, our city will no longer be a great place to live. It will no longer be a beautiful place for people to visit.

A concerned citizen,

Devin Jones

GO ON →

Now answer Numbers 1 through 5. Base your answers on "Let's Lose the Litter."

1 Read the sentence from the letter.

This is what happens when trash is <u>improperly</u> thrown away.

If *properly* means "correctly," what does the word <u>improperly</u> mean?

(A) knowing the correct way

(B) not done in a correct way

(C) not needing to correct something

(D) knowing how to correct something

2 This question has two parts. First, answer part A. Then, answer part B.

Part A: Which sentence **best** explains the author's point of view on teaching people not to litter?

(A) Everyone should help decorate the city.

(B) We should not worry about people who litter.

(C) The city should get involved to help stop littering.

(D) People who litter should be sent to other cities to help clean up.

Part B: Which sentence from the letter **best** supports your answer in part A?

(A) "We need to start a city program to clean up the litter."

(B) "One group called the Trash Masters picks up trash along its island's roads."

(C) "In Philadelphia, they say 'UnLitter Us.'"

(D) "It can teach people not to litter and it can also be fun."

GO ON →

3 Which text evidence supports the author's view that picking up litter is only one solution to litter? Pick **two** choices.

(A) "People have joined together in other places to pick up litter."

(B) "Litter can dirty our water and harm wildlife and the places where animals live."

(C) "We should also keep people from littering in the first place."

(D) "The next step is to teach people not to litter."

(E) "Stopping litter is not an unreachable goal."

(F) "It will no longer be a beautiful place for people to visit."

4 This question has two parts. First, answer part A. Then, answer part B.

Part A: Read the sentence from the letter.

If we are <u>unsuccessful</u> in stopping litter, our city will no longer be a great place to live.

What does the word <u>unsuccessful</u> **most likely** mean?

(A) Something has failed.

(B) Something has ended.

(C) Something has spread.

(D) Something has started.

Part B: Which word has the **same** suffix as the word <u>unsuccessful</u>?

(A) accessed

(B) careful

(C) recesses

(D) unsure

GO ON →

5 Complete the chart by writing the author's point of view about littering and the supporting details in the correct boxes. Use all of the sentences.

Author's Point of View	
Supporting Details	

Sentences:
City posters tell people not to litter.
Caring for our environment is important.
People can start a program to stop littering.
The city could provide more trash cans on streets.

GO ON →

Read the article "Community Gardens" before answering Numbers 6 through 10.

Community Gardens

In 1977, in a poor neighborhood of New York City, people noticed something surprising. It was there in a vacant lot. It wasn't the heaps of garbage or the old rusty cars, but rather the tomato plants that were growing wild. They looked unnatural, growing among the trash and tall buildings. "If vegetable plants can grow there," some of the people thought, "why can't we plant vegetables ourselves?" So the people cleared away the garbage and began growing vegetables, fruits, herbs, and even flowers. The Clinton Community Garden was started.

It is not alone, for community gardens are found in cities all around the country. People start community gardens in vacant lots. They plant them on apartment balconies. As unbelievable as it sounds, they even tend gardens on rooftops.

What exactly is a community garden? It's a garden that different people in a neighborhood plant and tend. It does not belong to any one person. Community gardeners eat and sometimes share the food they grow. Some community gardeners donate their food to local food banks that give it to people who cannot afford to buy all the food they need.

Some community gardens are one large plot of land. Everyone shares in the work. Everyone tills the whole plot to prepare the soil. They all plant seeds or young plants, weed, water, and share in the rewards. In other community gardens, the larger piece of land is divided up. People tend their own individual plots.

GO ON →

Community gardens are a great idea that offers many benefits. For one thing, they bring people together. Instead of remaining strangers, community gardeners get to know each other. Older people work alongside kids. Another benefit is the low-cost food, of course. The vegetables and fruits are also fresher and more healthful. And people tending a garden are getting fresh air and exercise.

In fact, a community garden benefits the whole community, not just the gardeners. It makes the neighborhood more beautiful. There can be no disagreement about that. Who doesn't find a garden lovelier to look at than a vacant lot? A community garden creates a green space among concrete streets and sidewalks. This helps reduce heat in the summer because the plants soak up sunlight. Concrete, on the other hand, reflects the sun's heat back into the air. Community gardens indirectly help save fuel resources too. Trucks don't have to deliver as much food from long distances to grocery stores. People don't have to drive as much to grocery stores, so less gas is used.

More community gardens should be started. With all the benefits they bring us, who could argue with that?

Now answer Numbers 6 through 10. Base your answers on "Community Gardens."

6 This question has two parts. First, answer part A. Then, answer part B.

Part A: Read the sentence from the article.

As <u>unbelievable</u> as it sounds, they even tend gardens on rooftops.

Which **best** describes an <u>unbelievable</u> idea?

(A) one that is not possible

(B) one that is based on facts

(C) one that is likely to happen

(D) one that is based on history

Part B: Which word has the **same** prefix as <u>unbelievable</u>?

(A) alive

(B) believing

(C) lovable

(D) undo

GO ON →

7 With which statements would the author **most likely** agree? Pick **two** choices.

(A) Community gardens help in different ways.

(B) Community gardens should replace city shops.

(C) Community gardens can solve most city problems.

(D) Community gardens are not helpful in some cities.

(E) Community gardens can help people make friends.

(F) Community gardens are better than regular gardens.

8 This question has two parts. First, answer part A. Then, answer part B.

Part A: Which statement **best** explains the author's view of a community garden?

(A) It belongs in the country.

(B) It should be used to make money.

(C) It should be planted on balconies.

(D) It can be used to feed many people.

Part B: Which sentence from the article **best** supports your answer in part A?

(A) "Community gardeners eat and sometimes share the food they grow."

(B) "Everyone tills the whole plot to prepare the soil."

(C) "For one thing, they bring people together."

(D) "The vegetables and fruits are also fresher and more healthful."

GO ON →

9 Read the sentence from the article.

There can be no <u>disagreement</u> about that.

What does the word <u>disagreement</u> **most likely** suggest?

Ⓐ taking action

Ⓑ getting along

Ⓒ not taking action

Ⓓ not getting along

10 Complete the chart below to show **one** cause from the article and **one** effect. Choose the correct sentences from the list below and write them in the chart.

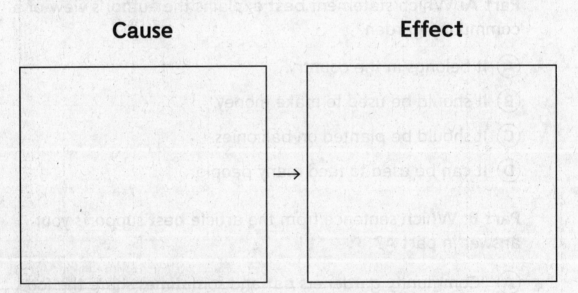

Cause   **Effect**

Causes and Effects:
Community gardens help save fuel.
People get to know other people on their block.
Community gardens help reduce heat in the summer.
Trucks and cars are not driven to the grocery store as much.

Name: _____ Date: _____

**Now answer Number 11. Base your answer on "Let's Lose the Litter"
and "Community Gardens."**

11 How do the authors of the articles feel about the way a city
should look to people? Include information from both articles to
support your answer.

_____

_____

_____

_____

_____

_____

_____

_____

_____

_____

_____

_____

_____

_____

_____

Question	Correct Answer	Content Focus	CCSS	Complexity
1	B	Prefixes and Suffixes	L.3.4b	DOK 1
2A	C	Author's Point of View	RI.3.6	DOK 3
2B	A	Author's Point of View/ Text Evidence	RI.3.6/ RI.3.1	DOK 3
3	C, D	Author's Point of View	RI.3.6	DOK 3
4A	A	Prefixes and Suffixes	L.3.4b	DOK 1
4B	B	Prefixes and Suffixes/Text Evidence	L.3.4b/ RI.3.1	DOK 1
5	see below	Author's Point of View	RI.3.6	DOK 3
6A	A	Prefixes and Suffixes	L.3.4b	DOK 1
6B	D	Prefixes and Suffixes/Text Evidence	L.3.4b/ RI.3.1	DOK 1
7	A, E	Author's Point of View	RI.3.6	DOK 3
8A	D	Author's Point of View	RI.3.6	DOK 3
8B	A	Author's Point of View/ Text Evidence	RI.3.6/ RI.3.1	DOK 3
9	D	Prefixes and Suffixes	L.3.4b	DOK 1
10	see below	Cause and Effect	RI.3.3	DOK 2
11	see below	Writing About Text	W.3.8	DOK 4

Comprehension 2A, 2B, 3, 5, 7, 8A, 8B, 10	/12		%
Vocabulary 1, 4A, 4B, 6A, 6B, 9	/8		%
Total Weekly Assessment Score	/20		%

5   Students should complete the chart with the following details:
- Author's Point of View—Caring for our environment is important.
- Supporting Details—City posters tell people not to litter.; People can start a program to stop littering.; The city could provide more trash cans on streets.

10   Students should complete the chart with the following cause and effect:
- Cause—Trucks and cars are not driven to the grocery store as much.
- Effect—Community gardens help to save fuel.

11   To receive full credit for the response, the following information should be included: Both authors feel that the way a city looks to people is important. The author of "Let's Lose the Litter" says that litter looks ugly. The author of "Community Gardens" says that one of the benefits of the gardens is that they make the neighborhood look beautiful.

Read the article "The Energy of Sound" before answering Numbers 1 through 5.

The Energy of Sound

Crash! Ping! Hiss! Creak! Woof!

Sounds surround us. Some sounds are enjoyable. Think of the song of a bird, the babble of a creek, or a piece of beautiful music. Each makes us smile. Other sounds are anything *but* enjoyable. When the brakes on a car screech, we shiver. When a mosquito buzzes unpleasantly in our ear, we want to run. When a jackhammer loudly rattles, we cover our ears. Yet the birdsong, the babble, the music, the screech, the buzz, and the rattle all have one thing in common. They are all a form of energy.

Sound travels through air as a wave of energy. A sound wave is caused when matter moves back and forth very quickly. This kind of quick movement is called *vibration*. When an object vibrates, it sends out sound waves. This is true whether the object is a singing bird or a buzzing mosquito. If all sounds are caused by vibrations, why do the bird and mosquito sound different? The difference is caused by *how* they are vibrating.

Sounds can be high or low. *Pitch* describes how high or low a sound is. For example, a whistle has a high pitch but a big bass drum has a low pitch. Objects that vibrate very quickly make sounds with a high pitch, like the whistle, but objects that vibrate slowly make sounds with a low pitch, like the drum.

Place your hand on your throat and hum. You will feel your vocal cords vibrate. Tighten your vocal cords, and they will vibrate more quickly. The pitch of your hum becomes higher.

GO ON →

Sounds can also be soft or loud. Very strong vibrations make loud sounds and weaker vibrations make softer or quieter sounds. Lightly tap a drum, and you will hear a soft sound, but hit the drum harder, and you will hear a louder sound. That is because the drum is vibrating with more energy.

Musical instruments use different vibrations to make different sounds. With a stringed instrument, like a guitar, you pluck the strings to make them vibrate. Each string has a different pitch. A short, thin, tight string vibrates faster than a longer, thicker, looser string, so it makes a higher-pitched sound. With a percussion instrument, like a drum, you hit the surface to make it vibrate. With a wind instrument, like a flute, the air you blow into it vibrates.

Stop now and listen. What sounds do you hear? Are they high or low? Are they soft or loud? Are they pleasant or just plain noise? Whatever they are, all the sounds are energy coming to your ears.

GO ON →

Now answer Numbers 1 through 5. Base your answers on "The Energy of Sound."

1 This question has two parts. First, answer part A. Then, answer part B.

Part A: Read the sentence from the article.

A sound wave is caused when matter moves back and <u>forth</u> very quickly.

What does the word <u>forth</u> mean in the sentence?

Ⓐ forward

Ⓑ into view

Ⓒ backward

Ⓓ after the third

Part B: Which word sounds like <u>forth</u> but has a different meaning?

Ⓐ farther

Ⓑ fast

Ⓒ fort

Ⓓ fourth

GO ON →

2 What does the author consider to be an enjoyable sound? Pick **two** choices.

Ⓐ a bird singing

Ⓑ a dog barking

Ⓒ a car screeching

Ⓓ a creek babbling

Ⓔ a mosquito buzzing

Ⓕ a jackhammer rattling

3 This question has two parts. First, answer part A. Then, answer part B.

Part A: Which statement explains what happens when something vibrates very quickly?

Ⓐ There is a low sound.

Ⓑ There is a high sound.

Ⓒ There is a loud sound.

Ⓓ There is a quiet sound.

Part B: Which detail from the article **best** supports your answer in part A?

Ⓐ "When an object vibrates, it sends out sound waves."

Ⓑ "*Pitch* describes how high or low a sound is."

Ⓒ "Objects that vibrate very quickly make sounds with a high pitch, . . ."

Ⓓ "Very strong vibrations make loud sounds . . ."

GO ON →

4 Read the sentences from the article. Underline the word that sounds like another word that means "separates into pieces."

When the brakes on a car screech, we shiver. When a mosquito buzzes unpleasantly in our ear, we want to run.

5 How does the author help the reader understand how musical instruments vibrate?

   Ⓐ by comparing the sizes of the instruments

   Ⓑ by explaining how to hold each instrument

   Ⓒ by comparing weak and strong instruments

   Ⓓ by explaining how different instruments are played

GO ON →

Read the article "How Do You Make Heat?" before answering Numbers 6 through 10.

How Do You Make Heat?

You know the sun makes heat, but did you know that you make heat too? You can make heat in some obvious ways by lighting a fire, turning on a stove, or turning up the thermostat. But how do you make heat in other ways?

If you've ever opened a car door after the car has been sitting in sunlight on a hot day, you know what solar heating is. The sun's rays enter the car through the windows. The more sunlight pours in, the more the air heats up. In a closed car, the heated air has nowhere to go. It stays inside the car. So when you open the door, the car inside feels almost like an oven. The steel on the outside of the car might be somewhat cool. But inside, the car seat might almost be untouchable! So, one way to make heat is to trap sunlight.

Did you know that you make heat inside your body? You make heat because you are moving and changing on the inside.

Everything that exists, including you, is made up of particles so small that you can't see them. These particles move because they have energy. The more energy they have, the faster they move. An object is hot when its particles move fast. The hot air inside the car got energy from the sun, so it has fast-moving particles. Slow-moving particles create less energy and cause cooler temperatures. Particles within a piece of ice barely move at all.

You have heat inside your body because your particles move fast. On a cold day, it's important to conserve this body heat in as much as possible. On a hot day, however, you want some of this heat to escape from your body into the air.

GO ON →

You also have heat inside your body because your body is constantly changing. Without food, you might feel weak. After you eat, you feel much stronger because food contains energy. When you eat food, your body breaks it down into particles it can use. Breaking down food also releases energy that, as you know, produces heat. The energy in your body helps you run, jump, and grow.

One thing you might notice is that when you run fast, you feel hotter. That is because when you use energy, you make heat. When you drink a cold glass of lemonade, the cold liquid enters your body. It slows down the particles, and your body cools down.

Have you noticed that rubbing cold hands together warms them? Rubbing causes friction, and friction is another way to make heat. The harder you rub your hands, the warmer they become. Thankfully, it's never hot enough to catch your hands on fire!

GO ON →

Now answer Numbers 6 through 10. Base your answers on "How Do You Make Heat?"

6 This question has two parts. First, answer part A. Then, answer part B.

Part A: Why did the author choose to use cause and effect in the second paragraph?

Ⓐ to show how the energy of the sun heats the air in a car

Ⓑ to show how important it is to keep windows open in a car

Ⓒ to show how we can solve problems by using energy from the sun

Ⓓ to show how air in a car on a sunny day is different from on a cloudy day

Part B: Which sentence from the article **best** supports your answer in part A?

Ⓐ "You know the sun makes heat, but did you know that you make heat too?"

Ⓑ "The more sunlight pours in, the more the air heats up."

Ⓒ "The steel on the outside of the car might be somewhat cool."

Ⓓ "But inside, the car seat might almost be untouchable!"

7 Read the sentence from the article.

The sun's <u>rays</u> enter the car through the windows.

Which is the correct definition for the word <u>rays</u>?

Ⓐ to build

Ⓑ to lift up

Ⓒ lines of light

Ⓓ an increase in pay

GO ON →

8 Underline **two** sentences in the paragraph that help to explain why an object becomes hot.

Everything that exists, including you, is made up of particles so small that you can't see them. These particles move because they have energy. The more energy they have, the faster they move. An object is hot when its particles move fast. The hot air inside the car got energy from the sun, so it has fast-moving particles. Slow-moving particles create less energy and cause cooler temperatures. Particles within a piece of ice barely move at all.

9 Read the paragraph from the passage and the directions that follow.

Have you noticed that rubbing cold hands together warms them? Rubbing causes friction, and friction is another way to make heat. The harder you rub your hands, the warmer they become. Thankfully, it's never hot enough to catch your hands on fire!

Why does the author explain the cause and effect of friction in the paragraph? Pick **two** choices.

Ⓐ to show the order in which heat happens

Ⓑ to show the problems of heating something

Ⓒ to show the difference between heat and cold

Ⓓ to show that there is more than one way to make heat

Ⓔ to show how heat is made when two things rub together

Ⓕ to show how there are many different temperatures of heat

GO ON →

10 This question has two parts. First, answer part A. Then, answer part B.

Part A: Read the sentence from the article.

Without food, you might feel <u>weak</u>.

What does the word <u>weak</u> mean in the sentence?

Ⓐ not strong

Ⓑ having force

Ⓒ lacking flavor

Ⓓ a period of seven days

Part B: Which word sounds like <u>weak</u> but has a different meaning?

Ⓐ walk

Ⓑ wake

Ⓒ week

Ⓓ work

STOP

Name: _____ Date: _____

Now answer Number 11. Base your answer on "The Energy of Sound."

11 How does vibration affect the sounds we hear? Include information from "The Energy of Sound" to support your answer.

_____

_____

_____

_____

_____

_____

_____

_____

_____

_____

_____

_____

_____

_____

_____

Question	Correct Answer	Content Focus	CCSS	Complexity
1A	A	Homophones	L.3.4a	DOK 1
1B	D	Homophones/Text Evidence	L.3.4a/ RI.3.1	DOK 1
2	A, D	Author's Point of View	RI.3.6	DOK 2
3A	B	Text Structure: Cause and Effect	RI.3.8	DOK 2
3B	C	Text Structure: Cause and Effect/ Text Evidence	RI.3.8/ RI.3.1	DOK 2
4	see below	Homophones	L.3.4a	DOK 1
5	D	Text Structure: Cause and Effect	RI.3.8	DOK 2
6A	A	Text Structure: Cause and Effect	RI.3.8	DOK 2
6B	B	Text Structure: Cause and Effect/ Text Evidence	RI.3.8/ RI.3.1	DOK 2
7	C	Homophones	L.3.4a	DOK 1
8	see below	Text Structure: Cause and Effect	RI.3.3	DOK 2
9	D, E	Text Structure: Cause and Effect	RI.3.8	DOK 2
10A	A	Homophones	L.3.4a	DOK 1
10B	C	Homophones/Text Evidence	L.3.4a/ RI.3.1	DOK 1
11	see below	Writing About Text	W.3.8	DOK 4

Comprehension 2, 3A, 3B, 5, 6A, 6B, 8, 9	/12	%
Vocabulary 1A, 1B, 4, 7, 10A, 10B	/8	%
Total Weekly Assessment Score	/20	%

4 Students should underline the word "brakes" in the sentences.

8 Students should underline the following sentences in the paragraph:
- An object is hot when its particles move fast.
- The hot air inside the car got energy from the sun, so it has fast-moving particles.

11 To receive full credit for the response, students should explain the role of vibration regarding pitch and volume. Very strong vibrations make loud sounds and weaker vibrations make quieter sounds.

Read the passage "A Riddle for Jeremy" before answering Numbers 1 through 5.

A Riddle for Jeremy

Jeremy always tried to be the best, no matter what he was doing. He had to win first place in the spelling bee, and he even had to shoot the most baskets in gym. However, Jeremy's biggest wish was to do better than his classmate, Chris Jones. It was not always easy for Jeremy to win because Chris liked to win, too. Sometimes Chris even beat Jeremy, but Jeremy would not get discouraged. He would just try harder the next time.

One day, the teacher made an important announcement. "The school wants to purchase several new computers for the library," she said excitedly. "We are going to hold a race to raise the money, so ask friends and family to help by making a donation to the school. I hope many of you can sign up for this event."

Jeremy knew that he was not the swiftest runner, but all he could think about was winning. He immediately decided to sign up for the race.

As Jeremy walked to school the next day, he saw Chris passing out fliers to his neighbors and friends that told them all about the school computers. Jeremy thought this was a waste of time. He just wanted to win so he could finally beat Chris.

GO ON →

Later that night, Jeremy asked his father to make a donation in his name. He could tell from his father's raised eyebrow that the answer was no.

"You are running for the wrong reason," his father said. "You should be running to help your school. Winning is not always a good reason for doing something."

"So?" responded Jeremy.

"Here is a riddle," replied his father. "If you run the race without collecting any money but pass the person in first place, who would be the winner?"

"I would be the winner!" said Jeremy proudly, for he was sure that he had the correct answer.

His father just sighed and shook his head.

On the day of the race, it was extremely hot outside and Jeremy could not wait to get started. Sand blew up from the track as the runners made their last-minute preparations. The gym coach called the runners to take their places. Then he yelled, "On your mark, get set," and the whistle blew. All the runners dashed forward.

Jeremy ran as fast as he could, but sand got in his eyes. He tried to run faster, but the finish line was still a long way away. He gasped for breath and his legs ached, but he kept running. Then he saw Chris, and his determination to win made Jeremy forget his pain. Jeremy sped up, and he quickly passed Chris, who had been in first place. The next day at school, Jeremy expected everyone to congratulate him, but instead, the teacher said she had some bad news. The race had not raised enough money to buy the computers for the school.

Suddenly, Jeremy understood the answer to his father's riddle. He had come in first place, but because he did not help to raise money, there was no real winner.

GO ON →

Now answer Numbers 1 through 5. Base your answers on "A Riddle for Jeremy."

1 This question has two parts. First, answer part A. Then, answer part B.

Part A: Which sentence **best** describes the lesson of the passage?

Ⓐ You should practice to improve your skills.

Ⓑ Winning is not the most important thing.

Ⓒ Ask an adult for help when you need it.

Ⓓ Always do your best in everything.

Part B: Which sentence from the passage **best** supports your answer in part A?

Ⓐ "Jeremy always tried to be the best, no matter what he was doing."

Ⓑ "As Jeremy walked to school the next day, he saw Chris passing out fliers to his neighbors and friends that told them all about the school computers."

Ⓒ "'You are running for the wrong reason,' his father said."

Ⓓ "Jeremy sped up, and he quickly passed Chris, who had been in first place."

2 Read the sentence from the passage.

One day, the teacher made an important <u>announcement</u>.

What is an <u>announcement</u>?

Ⓐ an action

Ⓑ an environment

Ⓒ a message

Ⓓ a thought

GO ON →

3 Read the sentences from the passage.

"The school wants to purchase several new computers for the library," she said excitedly. "We are going to hold a race to raise the money, so ask friends and family to help by making a donation to the school.

What do these sentences help to explain about the lesson of the passage? Pick **two** choices.

(A) Everyone should raise money.

(B) The school needs a lot of help.

(C) Running is the best school sport.

(D) The reason for the race is to raise money.

(E) The race is about more than just winning.

(F) Jeremy should not want to run in the race.

4 Read the sentence from the passage.

Sand blew up from the track as the runners made their last-minute preparations.

The word preparations has the root word *prepare*, which means "to get ready." When do you make preparations for something?

(A) after doing it

(B) while doing it

(C) before doing it

(D) at the end of doing it

GO ON →

5 Complete the chart to show how Jeremy changes in the passage. Write **one** word that describes him in the beginning and **one** word that describes him in the end. Then write the details from the passage to support your answers. Use the list below the chart.

	Word to Describe Jeremy	Detail from the Passage
Beginning of Passage		
End of Passage		

Words:

angry   selfish

aware   tired

Details:

Jeremy talks to his father at home.

Jeremy almost does not win the race.

Jeremy realizes there is no real winner.

Jeremy wants to win for the wrong reasons.

GO ON →

Read the passage "Pueblo Visit" before answering Numbers 6 through 10.

Pueblo Visit

Tisa was tired. Her family had been driving for two hours, and her little brother kept digging his elbow into her side. "When are we going to be there?" he asked.

Tisa's family was traveling to visit a Native American pueblo. All she could think about were her friends back home, playing. "Why am I in the back seat of this stuffy old car?" she whined to herself. "Who wants to visit an old pueblo? I have more important things to do today." Finally, her father pulled into the entrance of the pueblo, where Tisa saw a welcome sign. "This had better be worth it," she thought grumpily.

The scene before them made Tisa sit up and take notice. The village was nothing like her neighborhood, and the houses were nothing like her house. She and her family first walked into a wide open, flat area. "This is the plaza," her father reported, reading from a guidebook. A large, sprawling, brown earthen building stretched across the land beyond the plaza. It was stacked two, three, and even four stories high in some places, and bright blue doors dotted the building. "Each door marks a family's home," her father read. Wooden ladders led from one story to the next.

"Hmm," thought Tisa, "maybe this *will* be worth it."

The family strolled through the plaza and around the village as Tisa's father read them the history of the pueblo. "People have lived here for hundreds and hundreds of years. As their population grew, they enlarged the pueblo." On boldly striped blankets, some villagers had displayed their art for sale, and Tisa saw beautiful silver and turquoise jewelry. She especially liked the small clay figures of owls, cats, and lizards.

GO ON →

On this particular day, the pueblo was celebrating a holiday, and the people had invited outsiders to come and watch their dances. The dances were nothing like the dances Tisa had seen at weddings or parties. Women and girls danced in one line, while men and boys danced in another. Their outfits were trimmed in feathers and beads of every color. All the dancers moved to the low rumble of drums and the high-pitched chants of singers.

"Yes, this definitely *is* worth it," Tisa said to herself, smiling. She waved to catch the attention of a girl about her age, but her mother gently lowered Tisa's arm. "No, honey," she whispered. "This is a solemn occasion and we can't disturb them as they dance."

Later, the family gathered in front of a huge, beehive-shaped outdoor oven. They all watched as the baker lifted out a loaf of hot bread. The bread *was* a little like the bread Tisa was used to, but it tasted fresher and very delicious.

At the end of a long, eventful day, the family headed back home in their car. Tisa thought she might like to return to the pueblo another time. Perhaps she could meet the dancing girl. She would come on a day when the two could talk. Maybe they would become friends. Resting her tired feet, Tisa was glad she had visited the "old pueblo." She didn't even mind her little brother elbowing her.

GO ON →

Name: _____ Date: _____

Now answer Numbers 6 through 10. Base your answers on "Pueblo Visit."

6 This question has two parts. First, answer part A. Then, answer part B.

Part A: What inference can be made about the lesson of the passage?

Ⓐ It suggests that it is never too late to learn something new.

Ⓑ It has to do with being open to new experiences.

Ⓒ It teaches that you should always wear a smile.

Ⓓ It hints that you should never give up trying.

Part B: Which detail from the passage **best** supports your answer in part A?

Ⓐ Tisa is surprised to learn that she enjoys herself at the pueblo.

Ⓑ The people at the pueblo celebrate a holiday with special dances.

Ⓒ The family walks together through the plaza and around the village.

Ⓓ Tisa thinks about her friends while she sits in the back seat of the car.

GO ON →

7 Read the sentence from the passage.

A large, sprawling, brown <u>earthen</u> building stretched across the land beyond the plaza.

What is the root word of <u>earthen</u>?

(A) art

(B) ear

(C) earth

(D) then

8 Read the sentence from the passage.

Tisa thought she might like to return to the pueblo another time.

Which statement **best** explains how the sentence above supports the theme of the passage?

(A) by explaining that other people often share the same interests as you

(B) by showing that you should introduce friends to things you enjoy

(C) by explaining that you cannot always complete a task in one day

(D) by showing that you may like things you didn't think you would

GO ON →

9 Read the sentence from the passage.

"As their population grew, they <u>enlarged</u> the pueblo."

The word <u>enlarged</u> has the root word *large*, which means "very big." What does this suggest about the pueblo?

(A) The people added to it.

(B) The people knocked it down.

(C) The people moved away from it.

(D) The people divided it into sections.

10 Underline **two** sentences from the passage that support the story's theme.

"'When are we going to be there?' he asked."

"'Each door marks a family's home,' her father read."

"Their outfits were trimmed in feathers and beads of every color."

"'Yes, this definitely *is* worth it,' Tisa said to herself, smiling."

"The bread *was* a little like the bread Tisa was used to, but it tasted fresher and very delicious."

"Resting her tired feet, Tisa was glad she had visited the 'old pueblo.'"

Now answer Number 11. Base your answer on "A Riddle for Jeremy" and "Pueblo Visit."

11 What lessons do Jeremy and Tisa learn? How are the characters from both passages similar? Include details from both passages to support your answer.

_____

_____

_____

_____

_____

_____

_____

_____

_____

_____

_____

_____

_____

_____

Answer Key

Name: _____

Question	Correct Answer	Content Focus	CCSS	Complexity
1A	B	Theme	RL.3.2	DOK 3
1B	C	Theme/Text Evidence	RL.3.2/ RL.3.1	DOK 3
2	C	Root Words	L.3.4c	DOK 1
3	D, E	Theme	RL.3.2	DOK 3
4	C	Root Words	L.3.4c	DOK 1
5	see below	Character, Setting, Plot: Character	RL.3.3	DOK 3
6A	B	Theme	RL.3.2	DOK 3
6B	A	Theme/Text Evidence	RL.3.2/ RL.3.1	DOK 3
7	C	Root Words	L.3.4c	DOK 1
8	D	Theme	RL.3.2	DOK 3
9	A	Root Words	L.3.4c	DOK 1
10	see below	Theme	RL.3.2	DOK 3
11	see below	Writing About Text	W.3.8	DOK 4

Comprehension 1A, 1B, 3, 5, 6A, 6B, 8, 10	/12	%
Vocabulary 2, 4, 7, 9	/8	%
Total Weekly Assessment Score	/20	%

5 Students should complete the chart with the following information:
- Beginning of Passage—Word to Describe Jeremy: selfish; Detail from the Passage: Jeremy wants to win for the wrong reason.
- End of Passage—Word to Describe Jeremy: aware; Detail from the Passage: Jeremy realizes there is no real winner.

10 Students should underline the following sentences:
- "'Yes, this definitely *is* worth it,' Tisa said to herself, smiling."
- "Resting her tired feet, Tisa was glad she had visited the 'old pueblo.'"

11 To receive full credit for the response, the following information should be included: Jeremy learns that winning is not the most important thing. Tisa learns it is important to experience new things, such as a pueblo culture. Both characters are more concerned about themselves than others at the beginning of each passage.

Read the passage "The Weather Surprise" before answering Numbers 1 through 5.

The Weather Surprise

Andy glanced out the cafeteria window. The weather was warm and sunny, perfect for tomorrow's Walk-a-Thon. He, his friends Sasha and Jamal, and their parents were going to walk to raise money for the animal shelter. Sasha's older sister and Jamal's big brother were walking with them, too.

Still, Andy knew how fast the weather could change. "Sasha," Andy said, "there is a slim chance that it will rain or cold air might swoop in tomorrow. Maybe we should take our rain coats."

Smiling, Sasha said, "I think I will leave my rain coat at home tomorrow."

"Jamal," Andy said, "what if we wear shorts tomorrow and the temperature starts dropping? They will not cancel the Walk-a-Thon. It will happen come rain or shine."

Jamal smiled and slurped his milk as he said, "I am not worried."

Or what if it poured? They would all get soaked to the skin. He thought it would be sensible to take his umbrella. Sasha and Jamal were not planning ahead, so they would just get wet!

GO ON →

The next morning, Andy was still sleeping when he heard a loud rumble of thunder. He tried to look out his window, but it was raining so hard that he could not even see his back yard! They would have to do the Walk-a-Thon in a rainstorm!

Andy pulled on jeans and a shirt, walked downstairs, and grabbed his raincoat and umbrella out of the closet. Yet when he opened the front door, the sun was shining! His mouth fell open and he wondered how the weather could change so fast. Then he headed back inside and stuffed his rain gear back in the closet.

"How's the weather?" his dad called from the kitchen.

"Uh, good, I guess," Andy told him, heading back upstairs to change into shorts.

As he walked into his bedroom, Andy glanced out the window. Now it was snowing—a real blizzard! He raced downstairs and yanked open the front door, but it was still as sunny as ever. Then Andy heard a giggle from the backyard, and he tiptoed around the side of the house.

Jamal and his brother and Sasha and her sister were tossing bits of white paper into a big fan. The fan was blowing the bits of paper against his bedroom window so that it looked just like snow! A water hose lay nearby along with a metal trash can to make thunder, and Andy realized it was all a trick!

"Boo!" he yelled, and his friends jerked in surprise and then fell on the grass laughing. At first, Andy felt like blowing his top, but soon he was laughing too. He was not surprised when his parents came outside with big grins on their faces. "It was just a little joke, Andy," they said.

Andy smiled as he said, "I am beginning to think that the weather is not my biggest problem!" The Walk-a-Thon was a big success, and the weather stayed warm and sunny all day!

GO ON →

Name: _____ Date: _____

Now answer Numbers 1 through 5. Base your answers on "The Weather Surprise."

1 This question has two parts. First, answer part A. Then, answer part B.

Part A: Which sentence **best** describes the lesson of the passage?

Ⓐ People should do whatever they can to help animal shelters.

Ⓑ The weather will always be good if you are helping others.

Ⓒ Playing jokes that are harmless can be fun for everyone.

Ⓓ You will have good weather if you joke about it.

Part B: Which detail from the passage **best** supports your answer in part A?

Ⓐ Andy does not know what the weather will be like for the Walk-a-Thon.

Ⓑ Andy thinks it is snowing outside when he looks out the window.

Ⓒ Andy enjoys the jokes that his friends play on him.

Ⓓ Andy hears thunder while he is still in bed.

GO ON →

2 Read the sentence from the passage.

"Sasha," Andy said, "there is a slim chance that it will rain or cold air might swoop in tomorrow.

What is the meaning of the saying "a slim chance"?

(A) sure to happen

(B) likely to happen

(C) sure to not happen

(D) likely to not happen

3 Read the sentences from the passage.

Or what if it poured? They would all get soaked to the skin.

What does the saying "soaked to the skin" suggest about Andy and his friends?

(A) Their skin would itch.

(B) They would be caught in the rain.

(C) They would feel the rain on their skin.

(D) They would get wet through their clothes.

GO ON →

4 The passage has a message that friends play jokes to have fun with each other. Underline **three** sentences in the paragraphs below that support this message.

"Boo!" he yelled, and his friends jerked in surprise and then fell on the grass laughing. At first, Andy felt like blowing his top, but soon he was laughing too. He was not surprised when his parents came outside with big grins on their faces. "It was just a little joke, Andy," they said.

Andy smiled as he said, "I am beginning to think that the weather is not my biggest problem!" The Walk-a-Thon was a big success, and the weather stayed warm and sunny all day!

5 What does the passage teach about friendship? Pick **two** choices.

(A) Friends sometimes tease you.

(B) Good friends make fun of you a lot.

(C) Good friends share all of your worries.

(D) Friends like to laugh with one another.

(E) Friends try to help in any way they can.

(F) Good friends think the same way about things.

GO ON →

Read the passage "Finding the Farm" before answering Numbers 6 through 10.

Finding the Farm

The Abner family farm had always been a tabletop of green. The Abners grew wheat on the farm, and every year they harvested the wheat and sold the crop. The Abners were not rich, but they were happy. But then, in 1931, everything changed.

Dan was only nine when it seemed to stop raining. Clouds became as rare as hen's teeth. The first year, the grass only went brown and scratchy, but after the winter storms didn't arrive, the grass became dirt. The sun blazed down from a cloudless sky.

"We have to believe," Grandpa told Dan. "The rain comes and goes in these parts. Mark my words. Sure as Sunday the rain will be back."

First the little creeks dried up, and then the ponds started shrinking. They were mere puddles one day, and the next day they were nothing but cracked mud. There was nothing for the animals to drink, so Dan's father had to sell them. Though it was not usual, every so often the farm hands would come running across the pasture, screaming "Cloud!" and Dan would see one lone white cloud far off in the distance, but the cloud never held rain.

And then came the wind like a monster from another planet. It lifted the dust into a powder so fine it came easily through closed doors and windows. The Abner family farm blew into the air, and then it was gone. The black dust blizzards swept across the plains, blowing east. Cities hundreds of miles away were coated with the dust from the Abner farm and other farms just like it.

GO ON →

"It is over," Grandpa said, looking over the fields where nothing grew anymore. Everything was brown and there was no green to be seen. With no crop, there was no money, and soon there would be no food.

"What will we do?" Dan asked, uneasy and fearful.

"I believe it is time to leave," Grandpa said. "We have done all that we can here, and it is time to move on for our family is more important than our land."

But Pa and Grandma, and even Dan, who trusted his grandpa in all things, objected.

"You said we have to believe!"

"I still believe," Grandpa said solemnly. "I believe in the Abner family. We will go west, and that is where we will find the Abner farm."

So Grandpa, Grandma, Dan, and his father packed up their house and all their belongings. They loaded up the old truck and drove west. They followed the sun across deserts and limped over the mountains, and on the other side of the great Rockies, they saw the ocean. Clouds hovered over the water, and then suddenly it was raining cats and dogs. The Abner family got out of the truck and just stood in the downpour. Dan was soaked through to his skin, but he did not care. He tore up a handful of the soft green grass growing beneath his feet.

"I believe, Grandpa!" he shouted, laughing with joy. Then he and Grandpa tilted back their heads, opened their mouths, and let the rain pour in.

GO ON →

Now answer Numbers 6 through 10. Base your answers on "Finding the Farm."

6 This question has two parts. First, answer part A. Then, answer part B.

Part A: Which sentence **best** describes the theme of the passage?

Ⓐ Nature can be friendly.

Ⓑ Family is very important.

Ⓒ It is never too late to learn.

Ⓓ A good friend is hard to find.

Part B: Which detail from the passage **best** supports your answer in part A?

Ⓐ "The Abners were not rich, but they were happy."

Ⓑ "'The rain comes and goes in these parts.'"

Ⓒ "'. . . our family is more important than our land.'"

Ⓓ "They followed the sun across deserts . . ."

7 Pick **two** details that **best** support the theme of the passage.

Ⓐ The wind comes to destroy the Abner farm.

Ⓑ Grandpa says he believes in the Abner family.

Ⓒ The clouds disappear from the sky above the farm.

Ⓓ The Abner family supports Grandpa's decision to move.

Ⓔ Grandpa says it is over when he looks over the dry fields.

Ⓕ Grandpa and Dan open their mouths and the rain pours in.

GO ON →

Name: _____ Date: _____

8 Fill in the chart. Write the effect for each cause and the text evidence to support it. Choose from the details in the list below.

Cause	The rain stops falling.	The wind comes.
Effect		
Text Evidence		

Effects:

The farm dries up.   Dust blows into the air.

The Abners grow wheat.   The rain comes back.

Text Evidence:

"But then, in 1931, everything changed."

"Dan was only nine when it seemed to stop raining."

"And then came the wind like a monster from another planet."

"They loaded up the old truck and drove west."

GO ON →

9 Read the sentence from the passage.

Though it was not usual, <u>every so often</u> the farm hands would come running across the pasture, screaming "Cloud!" and Dan would see one lone white cloud far off in the distance, but the cloud never held rain.

What is the meaning of "every so often"?

(A) never

(B) very often

(C) sometimes

(D) all the time

10 Read the sentence from the passage.

Clouds hovered over the water, and then suddenly <u>it was raining cats and dogs.</u>

What does the saying "it was raining cats and dogs" mean?

(A) The clouds went away.

(B) It was raining very hard.

(C) There were cats and dogs around.

(D) Thunder sounded like cates and dogs.

Name: _____ Date: _____

Now answer Number 11. Base your answer on "The Weather Surprise" and "Finding the Farm."

11 What lessons do Andy and Dan learn? Include details from both passages to support your answer.

_____

_____

_____

_____

_____

_____

_____

_____

_____

_____

_____

_____

_____

_____

_____

_____

Answer Key

Name: _____

Question	Correct Answer	Content Focus	CCSS	Complexity
1A	C	Theme	RL.3.2	DOK 3
1B	C	Theme/Text Evidence	RL.3.2/ RL.3.1	DOK 3
2	D	Figurative Language: Idioms	L.3.5a	DOK 2
3	D	Figurative Language: Idioms	L.3.5a	DOK 2
4	see below	Theme	RL.3.2	DOK 3
5	A, D	Theme	RL.3.2	DOK 3
6A	B	Theme	RL.3.2	DOK 3
6B	C	Theme/Text Evidence	RL.3.2/ RL.3.1	DOK 3
7	B, D	Theme	RL.3.2	DOK 3
8	see below	Character, Setting, Plot: Cause and Effect	RL.3.3	DOK 2
9	C	Figurative Language: Idioms	L.3.5a	DOK 2
10	B	Figurative Language: Idioms	L.3.5a	DOK 2
11	see below	Writing About Text	W.3.8	DOK 4

Comprehension 1A, 1B, 4, 5, 6A, 6B, 7, 8	/12	%
Vocabulary 2, 3, 9, 10	/8	%
Total Weekly Assessment Score	/20	%

4 Students should underline the following sentences in the paragraphs:
- "Boo!" he yelled, and his friends jerked in surprise and then fell on the grass laughing.
- At first, Andy felt like blowing his top, but soon he was laughing too.
- "It was just a little joke, Andy," they said.

8 Students should complete the chart as follows:
- Cause—The rain stops falling; Effect—The farm dries up.; Text Evidence—"Dan was only nine when it seemed to stop raining."
- Cause—The wind comes; Effect—Dust blows into the air.; Text Evidence—"And then came the wind like a monster from another planet."

11 To receive full credit for the response, the following information should be included: Andy realizes that his friends play a joke on him to make him laugh and not to hurt his feelings. Dan understands that family is more important than what happens to the farm or where the family lives.

Read the article "First Journey to the Moon" before answering Numbers 1 through 5.

First Journey to the Moon

"This nation should commit itself to achieving the goal, before this decade is out, of landing a man on the moon." President John F. Kennedy made that pledge in 1961. That gave Americans less than nine years to reach the moon. What a challenge!

The country's space program needed to learn a lot more about space. A spacecraft needs to be launched at a very fast speed, and scientists worked at designing powerful rockets to solve the problem. They built rockets that could blast a spacecraft fast and far. Astronauts need to be able to breathe, eat, sleep, and work in space. Scientists worked at designing a spacecraft to meet these needs. They succeeded in building a spacecraft in which astronauts could live safely.

In the meantime, astronomers studied the moon. They knew the lunar surface was covered with dust, and some thought it might be so thick that a spacecraft would sink and be buried in it. Space probes were sent to the moon to take pictures and explore it.

Astronauts were carefully selected and trained. The scientists chose test pilots to be astronauts because test pilots know how to control a complicated aircraft. They are also very brave. The astronauts had to learn how to live in space with no gravity.

Then the space program was ready to send astronauts into space. First, an astronaut was sent into space in a rocket. He came back down in a small craft that landed in the ocean. The next step was for an astronaut to orbit, or circle around, Earth. Soon, more manned space flights took place. Some sent astronauts to orbit the moon. They did not land, but instead, they inspected the moon's surface and took photos. One crew looked for a safe place where a spacecraft might set down on the moon.

GO ON →

Finally, on July 16, 1969, a space flight called *Apollo 11* blasted off from Earth. Three astronauts were inside: Neil Armstrong, Buzz Aldrin, and Michael Collins. For more than three days, the men and their spacecraft drifted toward the moon before they orbited around it.

On July 20, Armstrong and Aldrin entered a small lunar lander called the *Eagle*. The *Eagle* left the main craft and began to descend to the moon's surface. Armstrong did not like the looks of the planned landing spot. It did not seem level enough. But Armstrong kept a cool head. He took control of the computer, chose another spot, and landed the *Eagle* safely. Then, inside the *Eagle*, the two astronauts ate the first meal ever on the moon.

A little while later, millions of spectators on Earth watched on TV. They saw Neil Armstrong walk down the ladder of the *Eagle* in his big spacesuit. His foot touched the dusty lunar surface. "That's one small step for a man; one giant leap for mankind," he said. The goal of putting a man on the moon had been reached eight years after President Kennedy's pledge.

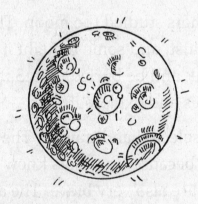

GO ON →

Now answer Numbers 1 through 5. Base your answers on "First Journey to the Moon."

1 This question has two parts. First, answer part A. Then, answer part B.

Part A: Which sentence explains the **main** problem facing America's space program after President Kennedy's challenge?

(A) There were not enough scientists.

(B) Few people wanted to be astronauts.

(C) They had more than nine years to do it.

(D) They did not know a lot about space travel.

Part B: Which sentence from the article **best** supports your answer in part A?

(A) "That gave Americans less than nine years to reach the moon."

(B) "The country's space program needed to learn a lot more about space."

(C) "They built rockets that could blast a spacecraft fast and far."

(D) "Astronauts were carefully selected and trained."

GO ON →

2 Read the sentence from the article.

They knew the <u>lunar</u> surface was covered with dust, and some thought it might be so thick that a spacecraft would sink and be buried in it.

The root of <u>lunar</u> is *luna*, which means "moon." What does this sentence refer to?

(A) watching planets

(B) landing on the moon

(C) discovering the moon

(D) traveling between planets

3 Arrange the events from the passage in the correct sequence. Write the sentences in the correct order in the chart below.

1	
2	
3	
4	

Events:
An astronaut orbits Earth.
An astronaut is sent into space in a rocket.
Astronauts orbit the moon and take photos.
The space program is ready to send astronauts into space.

GO ON →

4 Astronauts faced a problem in the lunar lander when they were about to land on the moon. Pick **two** sentences that explain how they solved this problem.

(A) The lunar lander left the main craft.

(B) The landing spot did not seem to be level.

(C) One astronaut did not like the landing site.

(D) The other astronaut found another landing site.

(E) The astronauts landed the lunar lander on the new site.

(F) The astronauts ate a meal after touching down on the moon.

5 Read the sentence from the article.

A little while later, millions of spectators on Earth watched on TV.

The root of spectators is *spect*, which means "to look at." What are spectators?

(A) people who watch something

(B) people who are often watched

(C) people who do not see anything

(D) people who like to look at themselves

GO ON →

Read the article "Early Sailors" before answering Numbers 6 through 10.

Early Sailors

Imagine you are sailing on a wooden ship long, long ago. The sky is darkening and the wind is howling. Huge ocean waves are swelling around you. The ship rocks up and down, side to side, and you see nothing but water in all directions.

Sailors long ago were brave. Many did not even know that the Earth was round. Some thought it was flat, and they feared they could sail off the edge. Others thought horrible creatures lurked in the sea. The ocean was a spectacle that held many dangers. Yet these nautical travelers explored new lands and brought goods to trade and sell. How did they manage to sail the world's waters successfully?

One tool they used was astronomy. For hundreds of years, people had studied the stars. They mapped the stars' positions and movements in the sky. With this knowledge, sailors could use an instrument called an *astrolabe* to help them figure out their ship's location. An astrolabe measured the positions of the sun and other stars above Earth. Suppose an astrolabe measured a certain star in a particular position. Then sailors would know how far north or south they were. If they measured the star in a different position later, they would know the direction they had traveled.

How could sailors know which direction they were sailing during the day? One instrument they used was a *compass*, which points to the direction north. A very early compass was made of a magnet on a straw or cork that floated in a bowl of water. The magnet would turn so that it pointed north. If sailors knew which direction was north, they could also tell where south, east, and west lay. They could steer their ship in the right direction.

GO ON →

Long ago, ships were not fueled by oil or coal, but rather they depended on wind power. Tall, wide sails would catch the wind, helping to move a ship along. Without wind, moving a ship was difficult. Early sailors noticed that certain areas of the ocean often have winds and they often blow in the same direction. They drew maps and made charts that showed these wind patterns. These tools helped sailors steer their ship to where the wind was blowing in the direction they wanted to travel.

Some of these winds are strong and steady. They blow the ocean water as well. The water flows in the direction that the winds blow. These flows of water are like giant rivers in the ocean called *currents*. Early sailors rode their ships on these currents, which carried them to where they wanted to go.

One tool used by sailors had a very special purpose. A brave sailor would climb a tall mast up to a small platform so high that it was called a *crow's nest*. Swaying back and forth, high above the ship's deck, the sailor would then peer through a telescope. The crew would wait for his shout: "Land ho!" After their many weeks at sea, land was truly a sight for sore eyes.

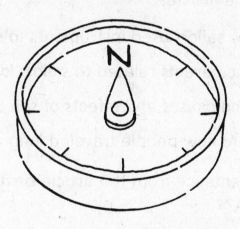

GO ON →

Now answer Numbers 6 through 10. Base your answers on "Early Sailors."

6 Read the sentence from the article.

Yet these <u>nautical</u> travelers explored new lands and brought goods to trade and sell.

The root of <u>nautical</u> is *naut*, which means "ship" or "sailor." What is a <u>nautical</u> traveler?

(A) someone who travels alone

(B) someone who travels on land

(C) someone who travels by water

(D) someone who travels with others

7 This question has two parts. First, answer part A. Then, answer part B.

Part A: What inference can be made about the third and fourth paragraphs of the article?

(A) They tell how sailors used instruments to solve problems.

(B) They sequence events related to sailors long ago.

(C) They show the causes and effects of sea travel.

(D) They compare how people traveled long ago.

Part B: Which sentence from the article **best** supports your answer in part A?

(A) "For hundreds of years, people had studied the stars."

(B) "They mapped the stars' positions and movements in the sky."

(C) "How could sailors know which direction they were sailing during the day?"

(D) "One instrument they used was a *compass*, which points to the direction north."

GO ON →

8 This question has two parts. First, answer part A. Then, answer part B.

Part A: Read the sentence from the article.

With this knowledge, sailors could use an instrument called an *astrolabe* to help them figure out their ship's location.

The root of astrolabe is *astro*, which means "star." What does this suggest about the astrolabe?

(A) It was used at night.

(B) It was used in airplanes.

(C) It was used during the day.

(D) It was used only a few times.

Part B: Which other words have the **same** root as the word astrolabe? Pick **two** choices.

(A) artist

(B) assignment

(C) astronaut

(D) astronomy

(E) labor

(F) laboratory

GO ON →

9 How are the ideas in the fifth and sixth paragraphs connected?

(A) by comparing the different tools sailors used

(B) by listing the different types of wind patterns

(C) by explaining how the sailors used wind power to sail

(D) by telling the order sailors followed their maps and charts

10 Draw a line to match the problem from the passage on the left with the solution on the right.

Problem

Sailors did not know which direction their ship was moving.

Sailors did not have motors or fuel to power their ship.

Sailors needed to be able to spot land from far away.

Solution

Sailors used a crow's nest to look out across the sea.

Sailors used the compass to guide them across the sea.

Sailors learned to steer their ship based on wind patterns.

Name: _____ Date: _____

Now answer Number 11. Base your answer on "First Journey to the Moon" and "Early Sailors."

11 How did space scientists and early sailors build and use tools and other inventions to solve their problems? Include information from both articles to support your answer.

_____

_____

_____

_____

_____

_____

_____

_____

_____

_____

_____

_____

Answer Key

Name: _____

Question	Correct Answer	Content Focus	CCSS	Complexity
1A	D	Text Structure: Problem and Solution	RI.3.3	DOK 3
1B	B	Text Structure: Problem and Solution/ Text Evidence	RI.3.3/ RI.3.1	DOK 3
2	B	Greek and Latin Roots	L.3.4c	DOK 1
3	see below	Text Structure: Sequence	RI.3.8	DOK 2
4	D, E	Text Structure: Problem and Solution	RI.3.3	DOK 2
5	A	Greek and Latin Roots	L.3.4c	DOK 1
6	C	Greek and Latin Roots	L.3.4c	DOK 1
7A	A	Text Structure: Problem and Solution	RI.3.3	DOK 2
7B	D	Text Structure: Problem and Solution/ Text Evidence	RI.3.3/ RI.3.1	DOK 2
8A	A	Greek and Latin Roots	L.3.4c	DOK 1
8B	C, D	Greek and Latin Roots/Text Evidence	L.3.4c/ RI.3.1	DOK 1
9	C	Text Structure: Problem and Solution	RI.3.3	DOK 2
10	see below	Text Structure: Problem and Solution	RI.3.3	DOK 2
11	see below	Writing About Text	W.3.8	DOK 4

Comprehension 1A, 1B, 3, 4, 7A, 7B, 9, 10	/12	%
Vocabulary 2, 5, 6, 8A, 8B	/8	%
Total Weekly Assessment Score	/20	%

3 Students should place the events in the following order:
- 1 – The space program is ready to send astronauts into space.
- 2 – An astronaut is sent into space in a rocket.
- 3 – An astronaut orbits Earth.
- 4 – Astronauts orbit the moon and take photos.

10 Students should draw lines to match the following problems and solutions:
- Problem—Sailors did not know which direction their ship was moving.; Solution—Sailors used the compass to guide them across the sea.
- Problem—Sailors did not have motors or fuel to power their ship.; Solution—Sailors learned to steer their ship based on wind patterns.
- Problem—Sailors needed to be able to spot land from far away.; Solution—Sailors used a crow's nest to look out across the sea.

11 To receive full credit for the response, the following information should be included: Space scientists built rockets and spacecraft to send astronauts safely to the moon. They used space probes to explore the moon's surface. Early sailors used tools like the astrolabe and compass to figure out their location and the direction in which they were traveling.

Read the article "The Smart Octopus" before answering Numbers 1 through 5.

The Smart Octopus

Scientists have known for a long time that chimpanzees are intelligent and that dolphins are very smart. Anyone can look at cats and dogs and tell that they have brains and use them. These pets also have emotions like happiness or sadness. They are playful, and each of these animals has its own personality. Scientists have found that an unlikely animal has been showing signs of intelligence: the octopus.

The octopus lives in the ocean and does not have a backbone. Its bag-like body and eight long tentacles flow along freely as it swims in the ocean water. Octopus tentacles have suckers along the bottom that can grab and hold things with great strength.

The octopus belongs to the same animal family as clams. Clams do not have brains and cannot move freely. They sit on the ocean floor inside their shells and wait for food to come to them.

So how did the octopus become so unlike a clam? Why does it have a brain? Scientists think that long ago the octopus once had a shell and no brain. Then, at some point, the octopus lost the shell. In order to survive, the animal developed a brain. For some animals, the octopus was prey. Without a shell, it had little protection from animals that hunted it. It also had to figure out how to catch its own food.

Not having a shell has its advantages. The octopus can move freely and hunt for its food. It can dart this way and that, and it might hide and pop out when a meal passes by. It can also swim and follow its prey in a high-speed chase.

GO ON →

In order to prove that the octopus has a brain, scientists have been keeping an eye on them for a long time. They have also performed tests. One test proved that the octopus knows the difference between two people. They put eight octopuses into a tank, and then two people came near the tank. One person fed the octopuses and the other one touched them with a stick. Within a week, the octopuses moved toward the feeder and stayed away from the person who annoyed them.

Another scientist gave octopuses puzzles, or little boxes with latches. The octopuses figured out how to open the latches!

One strange thing about octopus intelligence is that it's not just in its brain—the tentacles have minds of their own, too! For example, after an arm is cut off from the body, it will still look for food. When it catches it, the arm will take the food to where the mouth should be!

Only intelligent animals play, and the octopus is playful like dogs, cats, and other pets. It plays with toys like floating balls and plastic toys.

The octopus also knows how to protect itself. When it is resting, it will find an open place in the rocks where it can hide. An octopus has even been seen placing smaller rocks in front of its hideaway. Now that's using its brain!

GO ON →

Now answer Numbers 1 through 5. Base your answers on "The Smart Octopus."

1 This question has two parts. First, answer part A. Then, answer part B.

Part A: What is the **main** idea of the article?

(A) Scientists have proven that octopuses are intelligent.

(B) The octopus can be a very playful sea animal at times.

(C) The octopus is an interesting animal that has eight arms.

(D) Chimpanzees, dolphins, octopuses, cats, and dogs are smart.

Part B: Which sentence from the article **best** supports your answer in part A?

(A) "Scientists have known for a long time that chimpanzees are intelligent and that dolphins are very smart."

(B) "Scientists have found that an unlikely animal has been showing signs of intelligence: the octopus."

(C) "The octopus lives in the ocean and does not have a backbone."

(D) "So how did the octopus become so unlike a clam?"

2 Why does the author compare animals in the first paragraph of the article?

(A) to explain that scientists have not found any signs of intelligence

(B) to explain that the dolphin is the most intelligent animal

(C) to explain that many types of animals are smart

(D) to explain that animals have no personalities

GO ON →

3 This question has two parts. First, answer part A. Then, answer part B.

Part A: Read the sentences from the article.

These pets also have <u>emotions</u> like happiness or sadness. They are playful, and each of these animals has its own personality.

What does the word <u>emotions</u> **most likely** mean?

(A) beliefs

(B) feelings

(C) movements

(D) problems

Part B: Which words from the sentences **best** help to explain the meaning of <u>emotions</u>? Pick **two** words.

(A) pets

(B) happiness

(C) sadness

(D) animals

(E) own

(F) personality

GO ON →

4 According to the article, the octopus is **different** from a clam in a few ways. Pick **two** sentences that tell how the octopus is different.

(A) It has a brain.

(B) It is a sea animal.

(C) It has no tentacles.

(D) It can move around freely.

(E) It waits for food to come to it.

(F) It belongs to a different animal family.

5 Circle the word in the sentences that helps to explain what the word prey means.

For some animals, the octopus was <u>prey</u>. Without a shell, it had little protection from animals that hunted it.

GO ON →

Read the article "Wonderful Spider Webs" before answering Numbers 6 through 10.

Wonderful Spider Webs

Recently, a biologist found the largest spider web ever seen. It is also the strongest. The Darwin's bark spider spins giant webs that can be nearly thirty square feet. That's five feet tall and six feet wide. But the big web needs help to stay up. The strands that support these webs can be eighty-two feet in length.

To build a web that large, the Darwin's bark spider makes a super strong silk. This material is twice as strong as other spiders' silk. One reason it has to be strong is because the spiders spin them over small streams. Many insects fly over water looking for food. One web can catch thirty mosquitoes at a time. Scientists are still trying to understand how a spider the size of a coin can get its lines across a wide river.

The golden silk spider creates another amazing web. In the sunlight, its strands look like finely spun gold. The web is also super sticky. If you walk into one of these webs you will have a mess to clean up. The sticky silk is added after the spider builds a base of regular silk. These webs have to be taken down and rebuilt every so often because the stickiness wears out in the rain and when it collects dust. The spider actually eats the old web and reuses the material to build more webs.

Golden silk spiders also place chemicals on the web to keep ants away. They don't want other animals stealing their food. They build large webs in tree branches or on the edges of forests. These webs can be more than three feet across. The spiders also remove parts of their webs in high winds to prevent damage. These spiders make barrier webs to keep leaves away and protect the web from things blowing in the air.

GO ON →

Another fascinating web is the funnel spider's net. Unlike the golden silk spider, funnel spiders build a web shaped like a cone. It is small, less than six inches wide. Humans won't walk into this kind of web. This is a good thing because funnel spiders are very poisonous. They have to be because their silk is not sticky. Funnel spiders can feel a beetle or cockroach walking on their nets. Then they run out and bite their meal.

The spider hides inside a silk passageway in the middle of the funnel. It also creates "trip-lines" that warn the spider when something is near. Rain often floods these webs. Funnel spiders cannot swim. They are well protected under rocks or logs.

A spider's silk has amazing strength, so it is something humans want to use. Golden silk spider webs have been used as fishing nets. Scientists could rebuild parts of the human body with this silk. It is strong but also can stretch. A mesh of spider silk could repair damaged skin. Who knows what new ideas will dawn on scientists in the future.

Now answer Numbers 6 through 10. Base your answers on "Wonderful Spider Webs."

6 This question has two parts. First, answer part A. Then, answer part B.

Part A: Read the sentences from the article.

But the big web needs help to stay up. The strands that <u>support</u> these webs can be eighty-two feet in length.

What does the word <u>support</u> **most likely** mean in the sentence?

(A) prove

(B) remove

(C) hold up

(D) pay out

Part B: Which phrase from the sentences **best** helps to explain what <u>support</u> means?

(A) "the big web"

(B) "help to stay up"

(C) "these webs can be"

(D) "eighty-two feet"

7 How are the ideas connected in the second and third paragraphs of the article?

(A) They show why the Darwin's bark spider makes large webs.

(B) They show how spider webs are used to catch food.

(C) They show the problem with very large webs.

(D) They show how two spiders are different.

GO ON →

Name: _____ Date: _____

8 Compare and contrast the golden silk spider's web and the Darwin bark spider's web. Sort the details in the list and write them in the correct boxes in the chart. Fill in the chart with all of the details from the list.

Golden Silk Spider's Web	Both Spider Webs	Darwin Bark Spider's Web

Details:

Is very sticky

Looks like gold

Can be very large

Used to catch food

Made of very strong silk

Found over small streams

Often found in tree branches

GO ON →

9 Read the sentence from the article.

The spiders also remove parts of their webs in high winds to prevent <u>damage</u>.

What does the word <u>damage</u> **most likely** suggest?

Ⓐ loss of prey

Ⓑ catching prey

Ⓒ harm to the web

Ⓓ rebuilding the web

10 Pick **two** reasons why the author talks about different types of webs in the article.

Ⓐ to show how webs are rebuilt

Ⓑ to show how webs can be similar

Ⓒ to show problems caused by sticky webs

Ⓓ to show the way spiders build their webs step-by-step

Ⓔ to show how webs can be very different from each other

Ⓕ to show what scientists have learned about webs throughout time

STOP

Name: _____ Date: _____

Now answer Number 11. Base your answer on "The Smart Octopus" and "Wonderful Spider Webs."

11 How do the authors compare and contrast animals to show they are interesting creatures? Include information from both articles to support your answer.

_____

_____

_____

_____

_____

_____

_____

_____

_____

_____

_____

_____

_____

_____

Answer Key

Question	Correct Answer	Content Focus	CCSS	Complexity
1A	A	Main Idea and Key Details	RI.3.2	DOK 2
1B	B	Main Idea and Key Details/ Text Evidence	RI.3.2/ RI.3.1	DOK 2
2	C	Text Structure: Compare and Contrast	RI.3.8	DOK 2
3A	B	Context Clues: Paragraph Clues	L.3.4a	DOK 2
3B	B, C	Context Clues: Paragraph Clues/ Text Evidence	L.3.4a/ RI.3.1	DOK 2
4	A, D	Text Structure: Compare and Contrast	RI.3.8	DOK 2
5	see below	Context Clues: Paragraph Clues	L.3.4a	DOK 2
6A	C	Context Clues: Paragraph Clues	L.3.4a	DOK 2
6B	B	Context Clues: Paragraph Clues/ Text Evidence	L.3.4a/ RI.3.1	DOK 2
7	D	Text Structure: Compare and Contrast	RI.3.8	DOK 2
8	see below	Compare and Contrast	RI.3.3	DOK 2
9	C	Context Clues: Paragraph Clues	L.3.4a	DOK 2
10	B, E	Text Structure: Compare and Contrast	RI.3.8	DOK 2
11	see below	Writing About Text	W.3.8	DOK 4

Comprehension 1A, 1B, 2, 4, 7, 8, 10	/12	%
Vocabulary 3A, 3B, 5, 6A, 6B, 9	/8	%
Total Weekly Assessment Score	/20	%

5 Students should circle the word "hunted" in the sentences.

8 Students should complete the chart with the following details:
- Golden Silk Spider's Web—Is very sticky; Looks like gold; Often found in tree branches
- Both Spider Webs—Used to catch food
- Darwin Bark Spider's Web—Can be very large; Made of very strong silk; Found over small streams

11 To receive full credit for the response, the following information should be included: Both authors compare the subject of their articles to something we are familiar with; octopuses are compared to dogs and cats; Darwin's bark spider is compared to the size of a coin, and the strands of the golden silk spider's web are compared to finely spun gold. The articles also build upon each other by comparing and contrasting with other information provided in each text.

Read the poem "My Mom's Brain" before answering Numbers 1 through 5.

My Mom's Brain

Inside my mom's brain
You'll find a thing or two
There's not much fun in there,
Just things for me to do!

I want to shoot hoops outside,
I want to play on the court before it rains
"Wait! Hold your horses," she says
She's got chores on her brain.

There's homework to do,
And trash to take out,
"Just do it and smile,
Now, don't go and pout!"

At dinner that night there's
Spinach and carrots to eat,
"Eat your veggies," she says,
HA! That will be a feat!

I want to watch a movie,
Mom says, "You have to sleep,"
"But there's no school tomorrow!"
"Hit the hay now, and not a peep!"

The next day I make my bed,
Straighten my messy room,
I sweep and dust, clean and wipe,
Like a tornado with a broom!

GO ON →

I can't read Mom's mind but
After breakfast we take the car
What's in her brain now I wonder
'Cause we are traveling far!

An hour later I understand
Mom's brain had hidden a spark,
Friends wait for me at the gate
Of the Great Water Theme Park.

If I drew a map of Mom's brain,
There'd be chores and stuff aplenty,
But I'd make room for a special place,
It'd be called "Surprises for Benny!"

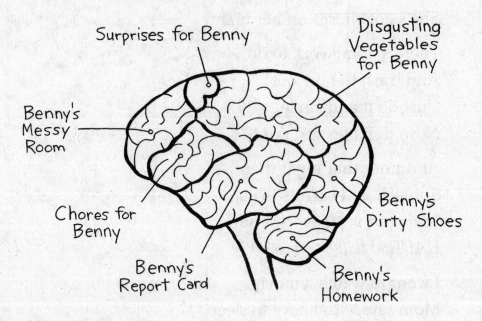

GO ON →

Name: _____ Date: _____

Now answer Numbers 1 through 5. Base your answers on "My Mom's Brain."

1 This question has two parts. First, answer part A. Then, answer part B.

Part A: Read the lines from the poem.

I want to watch a movie,
Mom says, "You have to sleep,"
"But there's no school tomorrow!"
"Hit the hay now, and not a peep!"

What does the saying "hit the hay" mean?

Ⓐ Go to bed.

Ⓑ Go to the barn.

Ⓒ Do your chores.

Ⓓ Do your homework.

Part B: Which phrase from the lines helps to show the meaning of "hit the hay"?

Ⓐ "watch a movie"

Ⓑ "you have to sleep"

Ⓒ "no school tomorrow"

Ⓓ "not a peep"

GO ON →

2 How does Benny **most likely** feel at the beginning of the poem?

(A) He thinks that cleaning is not fun.

(B) He thinks that his room is not that messy.

(C) He thinks that it is fun to take the trash out.

(D) He thinks his mother likes to plan fun things to do.

(E) He thinks that he should do his homework before it rains.

(F) He thinks his mother only thinks about chores for him to do.

3 Write the words from the list in the web to show how Benny feels in the poem. Write one word in each oval.

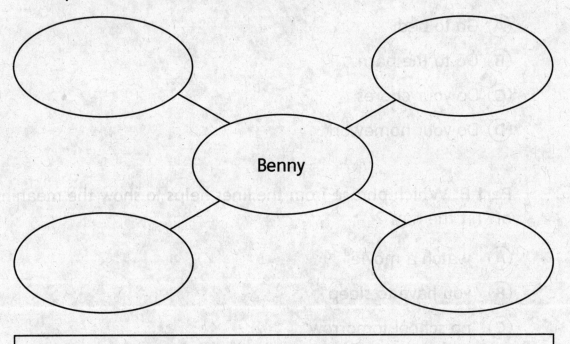

afraid	curious	happy	hungry
lonely	sleepy	surprised	upset

GO ON →

Weekly Assessment • Unit 6, Week 5

4 Read the lines from the poem.

I can't <u>read Mom's mind</u> but
After breakfast we take the car
What's in her brain now I wonder
'Cause we are traveling far!

What does the saying "read Mom's mind" mean?

(A) read his mother's book

(B) tell his mother what to think

(C) know what his mother is thinking

(D) know what will happen in the future

5 This question has two parts. First, answer part A. Then, answer part B.

Part A: Which statement **best** explains how Benny's feelings change at the end of the poem?

(A) He appreciates his friends who showed up at the park.

(B) He realizes his mom also wants to make him happy.

(C) He looks forward to doing his chores at home later.

(D) He wants to stop doing chores around the house.

Part B: Which line from the poem **best** supports your answer in part A?

(A) "An hour later I understand"

(B) "Friends wait for me at the gate"

(C) "If I drew a map of Mom's brain,"

(D) "It'd be called 'Surprises for Benny!'"

GO ON →

Read the poem "Hide and Seek" before answering Numbers 6 through 10.

Hide and Seek

Ellie the Elephant and Millie Mouse
Were bored one day
They had a terrific idea:
Let's find a game to play!

Millie said "Hide and Seek"
But Ellie said, "That's not fair."
Millie is tiny but Ellie is not.
She can be seen everywhere.

But Ellie loved Millie,
She wanted her to have fun,
So what if she lost the game,
An elephant was never glum.

Millie skittered away
She found a leaf to hide under,
5-4-3-2-1, here I come!
Ellie's walking as loud as thunder.

I might get squashed, Millie squealed.
That will be the last of me,
She left the ground to run straight up
The side of a banyan tree.

Ellie found Millie,
She saw her running up the tree,
"You don't hide very well, Millie,"
Ellie said with a lot of glee.

"You're a barrel of laughs,"
Millie said, "Now it's your turn to hide."
Millie knew she could find big Ellie
Even if her hands were tied.

GO ON →

A leopard can't change its spots,
And Ellie can't change her size,
But what Ellie did do you'll find
Came as a big surprise.

"5-4-3-2-1, here I come!"
Millie was ready for fun.
It would be as easy as pie
Finding Ellie who weighed a ton.

Millie found a gray mountain
It was a great place to climb
She would get to the top
Then Ellie would be easy to find.

Mouse looked up and down,
High and low she gazed,
Ellie gave me the slip,
Oh, how hidden she stays!

Mouse climbed down the mountain,
She spied an elephant's tail.
Oh, no! Ellie has lost her end,
And tiny mouse began to wail.

Then Millie found an elephant trunk,
She saw a big foot and a toe
This is the best hiding she had seen,
Her approval began to grow.

Mouse tripped over a whisker,
Ellie let out a huge sneeze,
She rose up and she bellowed,
"I won that game with ease!"

Millie and Ellie are still best friends,
"That won't change," they decreed.
"But no more games of hide and seek,"
To that they both agreed.

GO ON →

Name: _____ Date: _____

Now answer Numbers 6 through 10. Base your answers on "Hide and Seek."

6 Circle the stanza below that tells why Ellie plays hide and seek with Millie.

Ellie the Elephant and Millie Mouse
Were bored one day
They had a terrific idea:
Let's find a game to play!

Millie said "Hide and Seek"
But Ellie said, "That's not fair."
Millie is tiny but Ellie is not.
She can be seen everywhere.

But Ellie loved Millie,
She wanted her to have fun,
So what if she lost the game,
An elephant was never glum.

Millie skittered away
She found a leaf to hide under,
5-4-3-2-1, here I come!
Ellie's walking as loud as thunder.

7 Read the lines from the poem.

"You're a barrel of laughs,"
Millie said, "Now it's your turn to hide."

What does Millie mean when she says Ellie is "a barrel of laughs"?

Ⓐ Ellie is round.

Ⓑ Ellie is funny.

Ⓒ Ellie is very large.

Ⓓ Ellie is laughing loudly.

GO ON →

8 This question has two parts. First, answer part A. Then, answer part B.

Part A: Read the lines from the poem.

Mouse looked up and down,
High and low she gazed,
Ellie gave me the slip,
Oh, how hidden she stays!

What does the saying "gave me the slip" mean?

(A) got away from me

(B) gave me a present

(C) failed to come to me

(D) handed me a piece of paper

Part B: Which word from the lines **best** shows what "gave me the slip" means?

(A) looked

(B) down

(C) high

(D) hidden

GO ON →

9 Which conclusions can be drawn about Ellie? Pick **three** choices.

(A) She hates playing games.

(B) She is annoyed with Millie.

(C) She really likes her friend Millie.

(D) She does not like playing hide and seek.

(E) She wishes she were smaller than Millie.

(F) She thinks Millie is more important than a game.

10 This question has two parts. First, answer part A. Then, answer part B.

Part A: Which sentence **best** describes the lesson of the poem?

(A) Tricking a friend can be a lot of fun.

(B) Time with friends should be enjoyed.

(C) Some friends are more helpful than others.

(D) Good friends should talk to work out problems.

Part B: Which detail **best** supports your answer in part A?

(A) Millie does not find Ellie.

(B) Millie decides not to hide under a leaf.

(C) Ellie finds Millie when she runs up a tree.

(D) Ellie does what Millie wants to make her happy.

Now answer Number 11. Base your answer on "My Mom's Brain" and "Hide and Seek."

11 In both poems, the characters do something they do not want to do. What do the characters in each poem do? How are the characters similar? Include details from "both poems" to support your answer.

_____

_____

_____

_____

_____

_____

_____

_____

_____

_____

_____

_____

_____

Question	Correct Answer	Content Focus	CCSS	Complexity
1A	A	Figurative Language: Idioms	L.3.5a	DOK 2
1B	B	Figurative Language: Idioms/Text Evidence	L.3.5a/ RL.3.1	DOK 2
2	A, F	Point of View	RL.3.6	DOK 3
3	see below	Point of View	RL.3.6	DOK 3
4	C	Figurative Language: Idioms	L.3.5a	DOK 2
5A	B	Point of View	RL.3.6	DOK 3
5B	D	Point of View/Text Evidence	RL.3.6/ RL.3.1	DOK 3
6	see below	Point of View	RL.3.6	DOK 3
7	B	Figurative Language: Idioms	L.3.5a	DOK 2
8A	A	Figurative Language: Idioms	L.3.5a	DOK 2
8B	D	Figurative Language: Idioms/Text Evidence	L.3.5a/ RL.3.1	DOK 2
9	C, D, F	Point of View	RL.3.6	DOK 3
10A	B	Theme	RL.3.2	DOK 3
10B	D	Theme/Text Evidence	RL.3.2/ RL.3.1	DOK 3
11	see below	Writing About Text	W.3.8	DOK 4

Comprehension 2, 3, 5A, 5B, 6, 9, 10A, 10B		/12	%
Vocabulary 1A, 1B, 4, 7, 8A, 8B		/8	%
Total Weekly Assessment Score		/20	%

3 Students should complete the web with the following words to describe Benny:
- curious
- happy
- surprised
- upset

6 Students should circle the following stanza:
- But Ellie loved Millie,
  She wanted her to have fun,
  So what if she lost the game,
  An elephant was never glum.

11 To receive full credit for the response, the following information should be included: Benny does chores around the house and obeys his mom. Ellie plays a game of Hide and Seek with Millie. Benny listens to his mom and Ellie plays Hide and Seek because they both want to make someone else happy.